From Christ to Constan...
The Trial and Testimony
of the Early Church

Ken Curtis / Carsten Peter Thiede (Eds.)

Christian History Institute
Worcester, Pennsylvania

Pictures:
Datafoto International, Bunschoten: 1, 9, 13, 15, 16, 17, 18, 25, 27, 28, 31, 32, 33, 35, 40, 41, 42, 43, 44, 46, 47, 48, 50, 62, 65, 65, 66, 67, 68, 69, 70, 71, 72, 73, 74, 76, 77, 78, 79, 80, 81, 82, 83, 84, 85, 87, 89, 90, 91, 92, 94, 95, 97, 98, 99, 101, 104, 109, 115, 125, 130, 133, 134, 135, 136, 137, 139, 140, 142, 143, 144, 149, 150, 157, 159, 160.

Carsten Peter Thiede, Wuppertal: 2, 3, 4, 5, 7, 8, 10, 11, 14, 19, 20, 21, 22, 24, 26, 34, 38, 39, 45, 49, 58, 59, 61, 63, 75, 86, 88, 93, 100, 102, 111, 112, 113, 114, 116, 117, 120, 121, 122, 123, 124, 126, 127, 128, 129, 131, 132, 138, 141, 145, 146, 147, 151, 152, 153, 154, 154, 155, 156, 158.

Ken Curtis, Worcester: 106, 107, 108, back cover.

Günther S. Wegener, Zierenberg: 51, 55, 56, 118.

François Traudisch, Neuendettelsau: 23, 60.

Christoph Schilling, Gomaringen: 29, 30.

Rainer Riesner, Dußlingen: 6.

Beuroner Kunstverlag: 36.

Ashmolean Museum, Oxford: 53.

David Rubinger, Jerusalem: 54.

Martin Brändl, Tübingen: 103.

G. Dagh Orti / Christian History Magazine, Carol Stream: 105.

University of Michigan Library, Ann Arbor: 110.

Egyptian Museum Cairo: 119.

Cover: The manuscript illuminator Abuna Shimon at St Mark's Monastery, Jerusalem (C. P. Thiede); Raphael, Downfall of the Gods, Vatican (Datafoto International); Christ as Teacher, Ostia Antica (Datafoto International); Aquaeduct at Caesarea (Datafoto International).

Title page: Scene of Eucharist, Catacombs of Priscilla, Rome (Datafoto International).

Contents page: Jerusalem, Old City Wall (Datafoto International).

Back: Roman soldiers at dusk, scene from film series *The Trial and Testimony of the Early Church* (Ken Curtis).

Sources translated and paraphrased by the editors, except for the following, used with permission: I.1., I.2., I.3b, II.2a+b, II.3a: The Holy Bible, New International Version (Zondervan); I.4, II.3c, III.2b, IV.1b, V.1c, V.2d, VI.1, VI.2, VI.3b: Stevenson/Frend, A New Eusebius (SPCK).

**From Christ to Constantine.
The Trial and Testimony of the Early Church.
Compiled and written by Carsten Peter Thiede, with Ken Curtis.
Edited by Ken Curtis and Carsten Peter Thiede.
This book is a companion publication to a series of six half-hour films of the same title. The series is available on both 16 mm and video and comes with a complete curriculum package. For more information, contact Christian History Institute, Box 540, Worcester, PA 19490, USA, Phone: 215-584-1893, FAX: 215-584-4610.**

Copyright © 1991 Christian History Institute and R. Brockhaus Verlag

English language edition published by
Christian History Institute
Box 540, Worcester, PA 19490

Library of Congress
Catalog Card Number 91-73260

ISBN 1-56364-200-X

© 1991 German edition published under the title "Kirche in den Kinderschuhen" by R. Brockhaus Verlag Wuppertal and Zurich

Design: Carsten Buschke, Solingen
Typesetting: vom Schemm & Müller GmbH, Solingen
Printing: Maten Cromo, Spain

CONTENTS

Introduction

What is Early Church history — and does it really matter? It sounds like the dry-as-dust academic subject it often is — specialists editing, analyzing, and discussing records from long forgotten times which do not normally cater to the tastes and requirements of the beginner, the non-expert, or the curious new-comer.

This book attempts to demonstrate how fascinating the first three centuries of Christianity really are and what they mean to us today. Concentrating on major people and events, it is an appetizer, an introduction meant to encourage further study and reflection. And together with its illustrations showing the very latest finds of archaeology, authentic sites in their present state, and rarely depicted works of art, it also represents recent knowledge about the periods portrayed.

There are three components that make up the design of the book: quotations from original sources (both Christian and secular) that begin each section and are always on a left hand page; color pictures that relate to the theme of the section; and commentary that links the pictures and sources.

You will note that, within the commentary, numbers are given in parentheses that are keyed to the number on the picture you should consult at that point. Thus we urge that you begin by reading the source quotations at the beginning of each particular section and then, while reading the commentary, stop and examine the referenced photography.

This book itself was developed to accompany additional resources — a six-part film series having the same title as the book, and a curriculum package that goes with the films.

Each of these resources (films, curriculum, book) were produced so that they may be used alone or in concert to provide an introduction to the Early Church for the non-specialist.

We intended that these materials be of use both to Christian believers and non-believers alike. For the non-believer, we hope to present a view of the Church in its earliest centuries that provides a fresh look at what is really the essence of Christianity. So many in our Western world have rejected a Christianity that has very little to do with what Jesus intended his Church and followers to be, or have been turned away by an unfortunate church experience as a youth that has kept them from ever seriously facing what it really means to be a Christian.

For believers we earnestly hope that this exploration of the Church in its formative period will not only strengthen faith but also provide a new appreciation for the incredible story to which the Church is heir. Sadly, a majority of confessing Christians today suffer from a kind of spiritual amnesia. But once exposed to our fascinating and perplexing history, and the great company of struggling believers that preceded us in the faith, contemporary followers of Christ often see the meaning of their church association in a whole new light and larger dimension.

This introduction to sources available for study of the Early Church makes us acutely aware of how much more we would like to have. But Christianity during the period we are considering was an illegal religion — we might say a radical, counter-cultural, largely underground movement — and thus did not leave the many monuments or voluminous records as we would have wished. At the same time, you will see that we nevertheless have many invaluable resources (and this book just gives a small sampling) that enable us to piece together a meaningful impression and picture of what the Church was like in its earliest centuries.

Your editors, one a German, one an American, worked together closely on the preparation of the resources mentioned above (films, curriculum, and this book). This collaboration required countless faxes, phone calls, and letters. But, more important, it also required several trips to key Early Church locations — a search for data and sources that inevitably turned into "pilgrimages" and provided experiences that we will cherish for the remainder of our lives.

If we had to select one memorable moment that stands out among so many from the locations visited, we are agreed that it would be the Garden of Gethsemane. As we quietly walked there late in the day we were struck at the imposing view from the Garden of the pinnacle of the Temple wall in Jerusalem that is still standing and would have been visible to Jesus in Gethsemane. The pinnacle is where Satan took Jesus and tempted him to cast himself down and be miraculously delivered. It dawned upon us how closely related, both geographically and spiritually, were these two great temptations. For Jesus to cast himself down from the pinnacle would have meant building his ministry on the spectacular — on demonstrations of power. In the Garden, Jesus had to choose again to build his ministry on love, sacrifice, and service.

Repeatedly, in the preparation of these materials, we were reminded of how many times the believers in the first three centuries had to face their own Gethsemane's and decide, as Jesus had to, whether to go forward in spite of terrible cost and sacrifice.

The Church today still faces the temptation and question of what kind of power it will seek to affirm and employ. From the pages that follow we see how the Church coped, struggled, survived, and spread over a period of centuries when it was largely powerless, humanly and politically. There is much encouragement and wisdom here for the Church today that feels increasingly oppressed and marginalized by increasingly secularized Western societies. The Early Church had so much less than the Church today but perhaps in other ways it had much more. It is our hope that the following pages will offer some clues.

Ken Curtis / Carsten Peter Thiede
Spring 1991

1. The Beginnings of the Church

A Command of the Lord
Luke, Acts 1:1-14

In my former book, Theophilus, I wrote about all that Jesus began to do and to teach until the day he was taken up to heaven, after giving instructions through the Holy Spirit to the apostles he had chosen. After his suffering, he showed himself to these men and gave many convincing proofs that he was alive. He appeared to them over a period of forty days and spoke about the kingdom of God. On one occasion, while he was eating with them, he gave them this command: "Do not leave Jerusalem, but wait for the gift my Father promised, which you have heard me speak about. For John baptised with water, but in a few days you will be baptised with the Holy Spirit."

So when they met together, they asked him, "Lord, are you at this time going to restore the kingdom to Israel?"

He said to them: "It is not for you to know the times or dates the Father has set by his own authority. But you will receive power when the Holy Spirit comes on you; and you will be my witnesses in Jerusalem, and in all Judea and Samaria, and to the ends of the earth."

After he said this, he was taken up before their very eyes, and a cloud hid him from their sight.

They were looking intently up into the sky as he was going, when suddenly two men dressed in white stood beside them. "Men of Galilee," they said, "why do you stand here looking into the sky? This same Jesus, who has been taken from you into heaven, will come back in the same way you have seen him go into heaven." Then they returned to Jerusalem from the hill called the Mount of Olives, a Sabbath day's walk from the city. When they arrived, they went upstairs to the room where they were staying. Those present were Peter, John, James and Andrew; Philip and Thomas, Bartholomew and Matthew; James son of Alphaeus and Simon the Zealot, and Judas son of James. They all joined together constantly in prayer, along with the women and Mary the mother of Jesus, and his brothers.

Luke, the first investigative historian of the Early Church, sums up the events between the resurrection and Jesus' ascension. There was not yet a "church" as such, but there was a command to build on a growing congregation, to be the witnesses of Jesus Christ "in Jerusalem, in all Judea and Samaria, and to the ends of the earth." That group of disciples — eleven at the time, and Luke gives us their names, were promised the help of the Holy Spirit in their attempts to evangelize the world. They would not be on their own. Their group was growing already. Those skeptics of the ministry in Galilee — Jesus' own brothers (John 7:3-5) — had come to

the faith; they and some women were meeting in an upstairs room, joining together frequently for prayer.

The Essene Connection

This upper room was probably located on Mount Zion, the southwestern corner of the city of Jerusalem (1). It was a densely populated area, and recent archaeology has shown that the Essenes were immediate neighbors of the first Christians. The Essenes, along with the Pharisees and Sadducees, were one of the most important Jewish groups of the time. Many of their purifying baths (*mikvaot*) have been found in that area, confirming the testimony of the ancient Jewish historian Flavius Josephus.

The Essene Gate, linking the Essenes' quarter with the roads to Bethlehem and Qumran, has been rediscovered (3). From a certain vantage point, one can see the tower of the Dormition Abbey in the background (2), just beyond which the traces of the "Upper Room" can still be visited today.

Tourists will not miss the so-called "Tomb of David" with its entrance right next to the Dormition Abbey (4). Actually, the historial tomb of King

David was never here but on Mount Ofel to the east. A crusaders' cenotaph (memorial monument) had been mistaken for David's tomb in the Middle Ages. Today, only a minority of orthodox Jews still believes David

is buried here. However, that mistaken tradition has helped to preserve the remnants of the first Christian assembly room. The outer walls (5) reveal stones typical of first-century masonry. And inside, the niche behind the cenotaph of "David," the space traditionally reserved for the Torah scrolls (6), is not directed towards the Holy of Holies on the Temple Mount, as is usual in synagogues, but toward Golgotha − the place of the crucifixion. So it seems that these early Christians (who were, like Jesus, Jews) subtly shifted the emphasis of their synagogue from the Temple to Jesus. According to archaeological evidence, this must have happened in the late first century, not long after AD 70.

Meeting Places

The original "Upper Room" above the synagogue no longer exists; waves of conquests left the building in ruins. The first-floor room shown to visitors today was reconstructed by Franciscans in the 13th century, complete with earlier elements and some beautiful stone artwork, as in the pelican's column (7), symbolizing the sacrificial death of Jesus. (This was based on the ancient idea that the pelican punctured her own breast to feed the young on her blood.)

Other buildings in Jerusalem may preserve meeting places of the first Christians. The Syrian Orthodox Monastery of St. Mark, for instance, is thought by many to be where the house of Mark's mother stood (Acts 12:12). While archaeological

corroboration is lacking, the monastery embodies a living tradition of another kind. The monks, such as the manuscript illuminator Abuna Shimon, still speak the Aramaic of Jesus' time. Praying with them, one can hear the Lord's Prayer as Jesus would have said it.

It helps to see the first Christians as real people, living in real times. To see oral and literary traditions confirmed by archaeology and historical investigation, should not come as a surprise nor should it be seen as a distraction from the Christ of faith. The beginnings of the Church are rooted in the reality of the buildings, the gates, the rooms, the items of everyday life, and the manuscripts we can rediscover today − as well as in the reality of faith and prayer.

2. The World Comes to Jerusalem and Hears the Gospel

Peter's Great Public Address
Luke, Acts 2:1-12, 14, 29-47

When the day of Pentecost came, they were all together in one place. Suddenly a sound like the blowing of a violent wind came from heaven and filled the whole house where they were sitting. They saw what seemed to be tongues of fire that separated and came to rest on each of them. All of them were filled with the Holy Spirit and began to speak in other tongues as the Spirit enabled them.

Now there were staying in Jerusalem God-fearing Jews from every nation under heaven. When they heard this sound, a crowd came together in bewilderment, because each one heard them speaking in his own language. Utterly amazed, they asked: "Are not all these men who are speaking Galileans? Then how is it that each of us hears them in his own native language? Parthians, Medes and Elamites; residents of Mesopotamia, Judea and Cappadocia, Pontus and Asia, Phrygia and Pamphylia, Egypt and the parts of Libya near Cyrene; visitors from Rome (both Jews and converts to Judaism); Cretans and Arabs — we hear them declaring the wonders of God in our own tongues!"

Amazed and perplexed, they asked one another, "What does this mean?"

Then Peter stood up with the Eleven, raised his voice and addressed the crowd: "Fellow Jews and all of you who are in Jerusalem, let me explain this to you; listen carefully to what I say: "Brothers, I can tell you confidently that the patriarch David died and was buried, and his tomb is here to this day. But he was a prophet and knew that God had promised him on oath that he would place one of his descendants on his throne. Seeing what was ahead, he spoke of the resurrection of the Christ, that he was not abandoned to the grave, nor did his body see decay. God has raised this Jesus to life, and we are all witnesses of the fact. Exalted to the right hand of God, he has received from the Father the promised Holy Spirit and has poured out what you now see and hear. For David did not ascend to heaven, and yet he said,

> The Lord said to my Lord:
> "Sit at my right hand
> until I make your enemies
> a footstool for your feet."

"Therefore let all Israel be assured of this: God has made this Jesus, whom you crucified, both Lord and Christ."

When the people heard this, they were cut to the heart and said to Peter and the other apostles, "Brothers, what shall we do?"

Peter replied, "Repent and be baptised, every one of you, in the name of Jesus Christ so that your sins may be forgiven. And you will receive the gift of the Holy Spirit. The promise is for you and your children and for all who are far off — for all whom the Lord our God will call."

With many other words he warned them; and he pleaded with them, "Save yourselves from this corrupt generation." Those who accepted his message were baptised, and about three thousand were added to their number that day.

They devoted themselves to the apostles' teaching and to the fellowship, to the breaking of bread and to prayer. Everyone was filled with awe, and many wonders and miraculous signs were done by the apostles. All the believers were together and had everything in common. Selling their possessions and goods, they gave to anyone as he had need. Every day they continued to meet together in the temple courts. They broke bread in their homes and ate together with glad and sincere hearts, praising God and enjoying the favor of all the people. And the Lord added to their number daily those who were being saved.

9

Christian art has often sought to symbolize the Holy Spirit to come to terms with its presence and with the event of Pentecost. One such example can be seen in the church of St. Peter in Rome (9). The present-day church was under construction when Martin Luther came to Rome in 1512. It stands on the walls and foundations of Emperor Constantine's church, which had been consecrated in AD 326 to the memory of the Apostle Peter on the site of his tomb.

Peter, one of Jesus' inner circle, was leader of the young Jerusalem community on the day when the Holy Spirit came upon them. His public address shows that he was a devout Jew, a convinced follower of Jesus the Messiah, and an able interpreter of the Scriptures. Those with him, and indeed the first Christian artists to embellish sarcophagi some 200 years later, never forgot that this great leader was a sinner, too – something of which he himself was all too painfully aware. Earliest portraits do not show him with the "traditional" keys, but with a cock at his feet, a forefinger pointing to his chin, aware of guilt, looking knowingly at Jesus (10). The threefold betrayal of the Lord and Peter's instant remorse are depicted to great effect. The earnest, sober stature of this apostle is seen more in medieval and later art (11).

10

vehicle by which to make inroads into the hearts and minds of their fellow Jews. And the consequences soon became apparent. The first Christian community in Rome was probably established by Roman Jews who had heard Peter's speech in Jerusalem. But there was also a more immediate impact in Jerusalem. Thousands repented, were baptized, gave their possessions to the needy, and broke bread in each other's homes, praising God. Such common meals, following the example of the Lord's Supper, soon became a "trademark" of the Christians and were depicted on frescoes in the catacombs (15).

11

An Unlikely Leader

It remains one of the astounding features of the early church that a man like Peter, with all his shortcomings and failures, could become the effective leader of a far from uniform community within a far from friendly society. Even the most eloquent orator would have thought twice about addressing a multitude coming from so many different places in so many nations. It is true that he and the others with him, knew that the Holy Spirit was there to help. But that was exactly it: the Spirit was there to help, not to do their work for them. The use of one of the most important Jewish feasts of the year (*Shavuot*, Feast of Weeks), an event celebrated by tens of thousands and accompanied by traditional rites such as a Bar Mitzvah (13), was an ideal

And we find this mosaic (14) at Tabgha, near Capernaum, where the risen Jesus ate fish and bread with his disciples (John 21:9-14).

Pentecost and Peter's address constituted the perfect launching pad for worldwide mission. They signaled the beginnings of that important combination so apt even today: testifying to the faith at home and taking the message abroad. The Christian's call to mission has never been confined to distant shores.

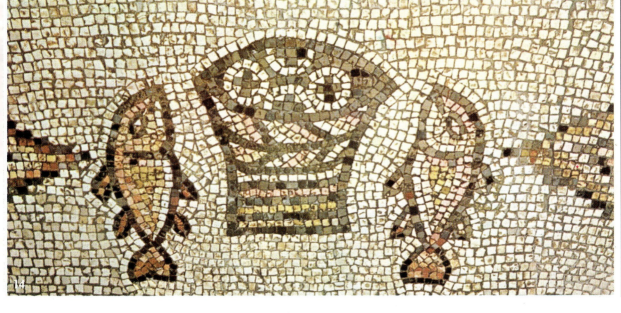

3. Mission Begins at Home

Peter at Caesarea
Luke, Acts 10:1-6, 9-16, 19-20, 24-29

At Caesarea there was a man namend Cornelius, a centurion in what was known as the Italian Regiment. He and all his family were devout and God-fearing; he gave generously to those in need and prayed to God regularly. One day at about three in the afternoon he had a vision. He distinctly saw an angel of God, who came to him and said, "Cornelius!"

Cornelius stared at him in fear. "What is it, Lord?" he asked.

The angel answered. "Your prayers and gifts to the poor have come up as a remembrance before God. Now send men to Joppa to bring back a man named Simon who is called Peter. He is staying with Simon the tanner, whose house is by the sea."

About noon the following day as they were approaching the city, Peter went up on the roof to pray.

He became hungry and wanted something to eat, and while the meal was being prepared, he fell into a trance. He saw heaven opened and something like a large sheet being let down to earth by its four corners. It contained all kinds of four-footed animals, as well as reptiles of the earth and birds of the air. Then a voice told him, "Get up, Peter. Kill and eat."

"Surely not, Lord!" Peter replied. "I have never eaten anything impure or unclean."

The voice spoke to him a second time, "Do not call anything impure that God has made clean."

This happened three times, and immediately the sheet was taken back to heaven.

While Peter was still thinking about the vision, the Spirit said to him, "Simon, three men are looking for you. So get up and go downstairs. Do not hesitate to go with them, for I have sent them."

The following day he arrived in Caesarea. Cornelius was expecting them and had called together his relatives and close friends. As Peter entered the house, Cornelius met him and fell at his feet in reverence. But Peter made him get up. "Stand up," he said, "I am only a man myself."

Talking with him, Peter went inside and found a large gathering of people. He said to them: "You are well aware that it is against our law for a Jew to associate with a Gentile or visit him. But God has shown me that I should not call any man impure or unclean. So when I was sent for, I came without raising any objection.

The Essenes in Jerusalem and at Qumran
Josephus, Jewish Antiquities, 18:18-22

The Essenes like to teach that in all things one should rely on God. They also declare that souls are immortal, and consider it necessary to struggle to obtain the reward of righteousness. They send offerings to the Temple, but perform their sacrifices using different customary purifications. Compared to all others adept in virtue, their practice of righteousness is admirable; nothing similar ever existed in any Greek or any barbarian even for a short time, yet among them it has prevailed unimpeded from a remote age. They put their property into a common stock, and the rich man enjoys no more of his fortune than does the man with absolutely nothing. And there are more than 4,000 men who behave in this way. In addition, they take no wives and acquire no slaves; in fact, they consider slavery an injustice, and marriage as leading to discord. They therefore live among themselves and serve each other. They choose virtuous men to collect the revenue and gather the various products of the soil and priests to prepare the bread and food.

The Jerusalem Christians did not wait for Paul's go-ahead to try and reach non-Jews. While "Jewish mission" remained their top priority, they still accepted opportunities to witness to others. Philip converted the Ethiopian treasury official (Acts 8:26-39), and Peter went to Caesarea, one of the centers of Greco-Roman civilization in Israel, to convert the whole household of the Roman centurion Cornelius. In each case, an angel of the Lord initiated the process. Peter, in particular, had been so deeply immersed in the everyday rituals of his Jewish upbringing that he simply could not bring himself to eat the unclean food of non-Jews — even if they were, like Cornelius, "God-fearers," who accepted Jewish precepts without becoming actual proselytes.

It must have been an impressive scene: soldiers, sent by Cornelius, escort the humble apostle solemnly back to Caesarea. The remains of that city, like the aqueduct (16/17) or the reconstructed theater (18), indicate the magnitude of the administrative center built by Herod the Great between BC 22 and BC 10 in honor of Emperor Augustus.

The Caesarea Shift

With Peter's successful visit, Caesarea became the site of the conversion of the first high ranking Roman to the Christian faith. Paul, too, knew

17

Caesarea well; he had stayed here before leaving for Tarsus, and he returned here after his second and third missionary journeys. Still later, Paul was under arrest here for two years before he was sent to Rome about AD 57. The harbor of Caesarea (19), parts of which are visible above ground, has recently become the subject of underwater archaeology.

Mission to the Gentiles was hotly debated among the very first Christians. Back in Jerusalem, the reaction to Peter's success at Caesarea was ambivalent (Acts 11), and Paul later had to support the cause of non-Jewish converts (Acts 15). The church was slowly moving toward a point where new Christians did not have to become Jews first. Again it was Peter who helped pave the way to a solution with his opening address at the so-called "Apostolic Council" in Jerusalem in

AD 48 (Acts 15:7-11). For a long time to come, Jewish Christians and Gentile Christians remained among themselves and met in separate house churches. Paul, who did not like this state of affairs at all (see Galatians 2:11-14), had to accept it in the list of greetings at the end of his letter to the Romans, where Jewish and Gentile Christian households are kept apart.

The Jewish Mission

Near home, mission among their fellow Jews was as successful as it was complicated. The Sadducees, who had always excluded even the possibility of a bodily resurrection (Matthew 22:23-34), remained aloof. The Pharisees were rather more open-minded. One of their number, the renowned leader Gamaliel, Paul's former teacher, showed signs of flexibility (Acts 5:34-39). Indeed, Paul himself had been a Pharisee before becoming a Christian.

The Essenes, the third major Jewish group, were a case apart. They are not mentioned by name in the New Testament (they did not call themselves Essenes anyway), but we find their traces more than once — John the Baptist, when he lived "in the desert" (Luke 1:80), probably stayed with the Essenes at their desert "monastery" of Qumran (20) south of Jericho, not far from the Dead Sea. The famous Dead Sea Scrolls were found here, some of which were written in a "scriptorium," the lower floor of which can still be seen (21). The manuscripts were found in caves such as these (22) near the settlement. The Essenes probably retreated here

from Jerusalem in the mid-second century BC, when conflict with the temple priests became insufferable. The complete scroll of Isaiah (23), over 22 feet long, remains a fascinating example of the faithful textual tradition they preserved.

Though the Essenes' sectarian writings contain many peculiar teachings, they also show some resemblance to early Christian thinking. Some scholars have assumed that the first Christians copied from Essene doctrine. However, Acts 6:7 hints that some Essenes from Jerusalem became Christians themselves. The "many

priests" who converted must have been Essenes, for the Pharisees were not led by priests, and the Sadducees, who had priests, did not even accept

19

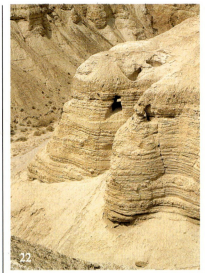

the possibility of any resurrection, as we have noted.

The neighborly existence of Christians and Essenes in Jerusalem, demonstrated by recent archaeology, gives rise to another line of inquiry: Why was the judgment of Ananias and Sapphira (Acts 5:1-11) so severe? Could it be that the Christians had to appear as strict as the Essenes in their rigid community regulations? If so, they succeeded. And it would be yet another example of Christians looking very closely at the customs of their "target groups" before beginning the process of evangelization.

4. Conflict and Separation: the Beginning Divide Between Jews and Jewish Christians

Martyrdom of James, the Lord's Brother
Josephus, Jewish Antiquities 20, 7:1

The younger Ananus, who had recently become the High Priest, was bold and very insolent. He was also a Sadducee − a Jewish sect known for being the most judgmental of offenders. Because of his disposition, he assumed he had the right to exercise his authority.

Festus was now dead, and Albinus was travelling. So Ananus assembled the Sanhedrin (judges) and brought James, the brother of Jesus (who was called Christ) and some others before them. He accused them of breaking the law and delivered them to be stoned. But some upstanding citizens who were aware of legal matters disliked Ananus' actions. They sent to King Agrippa, desiring him to forbid Ananus from acting against these men anymore because his actions were unjustified. Some of them also went to meet Albinus, while he was on his trip from Alexandria, and informed him that

Ananus could not legally assemble a Sanhedrin without his consent. Albinus was persuaded by what they said. He was angry and wrote Ananus a letter, telling him he would be punished for his actions. Then, King Agrippa took the High Priesthood from him after he had ruled only three months. Jesus, the son of Damneus, was then made High Priest.

Flight of the Christians from Jerusalem
Eusebius, Church History, 3, 5:3

The Christians of Jerusalem had been told by God in a divine revelation to depart from the city before the war. They were to inhabit Peraea, a city they called Pella. When these Christian believers left Jerusalem, deserting the royal city of the Jews and the land of Judea, God destroyed that generation of wicked persons − foot and branch − retribution for their acts of violence to Christ and his apostles.

The very first Christians were Jews. They did not see themselves as establishing a new religion or even a new sect or breakaway group from Judaism. On the contrary, they saw themselves as loyal to their Jewish heritage. They also believed in the promises given to Israel by God. For them, the Temple in Jerusalem remained the focus of worship: "Every day they continued to meet together in the Temple courts" (Acts 2:46). A sight like this one, visible today (24/28), would have saddened them as much as it has saddened all Jews to the present day. This is all that remains of the Temple complex where those first Christians met — nothing but a retaining wall, the so called Western Wall, which has been called the "Wailing Wall," not without reason. A mosque stands on the plateau where the central building of the Temple once was.

Conflicts arose when the Christian community used the Temple precincts for ostentatious actions (Acts

24

3:1-4:4). And when Stephen was falsely accused of "speaking against the holy place (the Temple) and the law" (Acts 6:13), the charge led to an impromptu trial and his stoning outside the city walls. Stephen, a Jewish Christian himself, became the first martyr of the church's conflict with

its fellow Jews, and later Paul nearly met a similar fate when he was falsely accused of having brought a pagan Greek into the Temple and people "were trying to kill him" (Acts 21:27-31).

The splendors of the Temple, reconstructed in this model (25), disappeared in AD 70 when the Romans

25

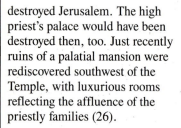

26

27

destroyed Jerusalem. The high priest's palace would have been destroyed then, too. Just recently ruins of a palatial mansion were rediscovered southwest of the Temple, with luxurious rooms reflecting the affluence of the priestly families (26).

A Way of Life
One of the reasons why so many in Jerusalem followed the Christians rather than the priests – beyond their message as such – may have been this different way of life. The Christians, sharing their possessions and

28

living modestly, led by unpretentious apostles like Peter and James, the Lord's brother, were more acceptable to ordinary men and women than the lofty priests of the Temple.

In fact, it was said that James prayed so fervently in the Temple that he had callouses on his knees, earning him the nickname "camel-knees." One is easily reminded of the relentless fervor of some of the orthodox Jews praying at the Western Wall today, day and night (27/28).

This James emerged as the central figure among the Jerusalem Christians after the murder of James, John's brother, and Peter's escape from prison (Acts 12:1-17). He stood strongly for the traditional Jewish heritage within Christianity. Thus, he was a major force Paul had to reckon with in his attempts to convert pagans without forcing them to become Jews first (see Acts 15). Apparently James achieved some popularity in the Jerusalem community at large, since his

martyrdom in AD 62 aroused vigorous protests even from non Christian Jews.

Fleeing to Pella

With James' death, the authoritative Jewish-Christian position began to wane. Four years later, at the beginning of the Jewish revolt against Rome (which led to the destruction of Jerusalem), the Christians left the city. Many settled in Pella, to the north and across the Jordan River. The site,

29

30

in modern-day Jordan, is being excavated by archaeologists (29/30). Nothing much of first-century Christianity has come to light so far, but the importance of the site is clearly shown by later Christian buildings. The site remained a Christian stronghold until the Islamic invasion of the seventh century. The historian Eusebius, writing from Rome around AD 315, saw this flight of the Christians from Jerusalem to Pella in AD 66 as a command and as a kind of seal on the separation of Christians and Jews. He even went so far as to regard the destruction of Jerusalem as God's justice visited on those who had mistreated Jesus and the Apostles. In Rome, he could have seen the Arch of Titus celebrating the man who had conquered Jerusalem and looted the Temple (31). And, carved into the Arch, Eusebius could have seen the Menorah, the seven-branched candlestick stolen from the Temple, and he may even have enjoyed this sight (32). But the rampant anti-semitism that shines through his words was not shared by those Christians who had left for Pella. They did not seek separation, and when some of them returned after AD 70, they tried once again to bridge the gap that had been opened.

32

1. Preconditions within the Empire

Father of the Fatherland
Augustus, Monumentum Ancyranum, 25-26, 35

I have pacified the seas; in my war against the
pirates, I took almost 30,000 slaves prisoner
who had escaped from their owners and had
raised up arms against Rome, and returned
them to their owners for punishment.

All Italy swore the oath of allegiance to me
and expressly asked me to be its leader in the
war which I won at Actium. The Provinces of
Gaul and Spain, Africa, Sicily and Sardinia
took the same oath.

I have enlarged the area of all provinces
where the Roman people had tribes as neighbors who did not submit to our rule.
I have pacified the provinces of Spain and
Germany, an area which the ocean encompasses
from Gades to the mouth of the river Elbe. I
had the Alps pacified from the area bordering
on the Adriatic Sea to the Thyrennian Sea, and
no unlawful war was waged on any people.
My navy went from the mouth of the river
Rhine across the sea to the land of the Cimbri.
Neither by water nor on land had Romans
reached this region before. The Cimbri and the
Charides and Semnones and other Teutonic
tribes from this area sent delegates and asked
for my and my people's friendship.

When I administered my thirteenth consulate,
the Senate, the Knights and the Roman people
unanimously bestowed on me the title "Father
of the Fatherland." They decided that this
should be inscribed in the hall of my house, in
the Curia Julia, and on the base of the quadriga
which the Senate had erected for me on the
Forum of Augustus. At the time of writing, I am
76 years old.

A Christian Appraisal of Augustus
Melito of Sardis, To Emperor Marcus Aurelius,
in: Eusebius, Church History, 4, 26:7-9

Our philosophy first grew up among the bar-
barians, but its full flower came among your
peoples in the great reign of your ancestor
Augustus, and became an auspicious boon to
your empire, for from that time the power of the
Romans became great and splendid. You are
now his happy successor, and shall be so along
with your son, if you protect the philosophy
which grew up with the empire and began with
Augustus. Your ancestors respected it together
with the other cults, and the greatest proof that
our doctrine flourished for the good, along with
your empire in its noble beginning, is the fact
that it met no evil in the reign of Augustus, but
on the contrary experienced everything splendid
and glorious according to the wishes of all men.
The only emperors who were ever persuaded by
malicious men to slander our teaching were
Nero and Domitian, and from them arose the
unreasonable custom of falsely accusing
Christians.

33

34

Each year in the Christmas story, we read, "…a decree went out from Caesar Augustus" (Luke 2:1). It is fitting that the story of Christianity begins with him, for Emperor Augustus (34) brought the dawn of a new age in Rome and the entire Mediterranean world.

His full name was Gaius Julius Caesar Octavianus. Adopted by Julius Caesar, "Octavian" avenged his assassination, defeating Mark Antony at Actium in 31 BC and becoming sole ruler of the Empire. The Senate bestowed on him the honorary title of "Augustus" in 27 BC.

Although he died in AD 14, long before the ministry of Jesus began, Augustus left a lasting imprint on the New Testament and early Christian period. He had achieved the consolidation of the Empire, the *Pax Romana*. In his honor, the Senate erected the Altar of Peace, the "Ara Pacis" (33), rediscovered and reconstructed by archaeologists opposite his mausoleum in Rome. On an outer wall, the autobiographical recording of his deeds, the so-called "Monumentum Ancyranum" (named after the place where it was found, Ankara, in modern Turkey), is a later addition (35). The

35

36

Latin and Greek text is an impressive account of his efforts to achieve and preserve peace within the empire and to protect its borders. Augustus, the "Father of the Fatherland," had created an empire where the seas and roads were safer than ever before, where people could travel freely and quickly, where tranquility prevailed at last after a century of civil conflicts and revolutions.

For those first Christians, whose aim was to take the gospel to the "ends of the earth," nothing could have been more convenient than a borderless realm stretching from what is now Portugal and Spain to Britain, West Germany, Turkey, Syria and Iraq, Egypt, and the whole of North Africa.

Patron of Poets

Augustus, for whom our eighth month is named, was far from perfect. His behavior toward certain members of his family, opponents, and critical poets was far from magnanimous. Some of the great poets of Rome, however, enjoyed his favors, Horace and Virgil among them. One of Virgil's poems, the fourth Eclogue, foretells, apparently for the year 40 BC, the birth of a divine child who would be the Savior of the world. This cannot have been Augustus himself, who was born in 63 BC, although he had been hailed as the "newly born ruler of the world" on the day of his birth, nor can it apply to any of his children. But in spite of the chronological improbability, it

was seen by many Christian readers as a prophecy of Christ's birth, and Virgil, who died in 17 BC, has been called "a Christian without Christ." In fact, it has been shown that Virgil knew the Old Testament in Greek translation, since he alludes to prophetic passages, such as Isaiah 9:6 and 11:1-8 in his fourth Eclogue. There is a statue of him, among the Old Testament prophets, in the Spanish Cathedral of Zamorra.

It may be an accident that a cameo of Augustus was placed in the center of the ninth-century Cross of Lothar (36), now at the Cathedral of Aix-la-Chapelle (Aachen) in Germany. But it is certainly true that historians have tended to regard Augustus favorably in comparison with later emperors. The second-century writer Melito of Sardis, in his address to the emperor Marcus Aurelius, quoted here at the beginning of this chapter, is a case in point.

Had they analyzed his religious life,

the verdict would have been much less complimentary. Augustus was not one of those who believed, as Plato had (according to his Christian interpreters), in the existence of God — known or unknown — but was exceedingly superstitious, using the traditional forms of Roman religion merely for political purposes.

Among the many remaining traces of his buildings in Rome, the great Forum of Augustus (37) still betrays the grandeur of his thinking. And even here, an element of Christian presence has since been integrated, for the building at the far end, on the left hand side, now houses the Italian Chapter of the Maltese Knights, who, with their Protestant counterpart, the Order of St John, have become known as "Hospitallers," caring for the sick and needy, and are the oldest order of knights in Christendom.

2. Rulers, Roads and Rival Cults

A Calendar of Rulers
Luke, Gospel 3:1-4

In the Fifteenth year of the Emperor Tiberius, when Pontius Pilate was governor of Judea, when Herod was Tetrarch of Galilee, his brother Philip Tetrarch of Ituraea and Trachonitis, and Lysanias Tetrarch of Abilene, during the high-priesthood of Annas and Caiaphas, the word of God came to John, the son of Zechariah, in the wilderness. And he went all over the Jordan valley proclaiming the baptism of repentance for the forgiveness of sins.

International Travel
Luke, Acts, 28:11-15

Three months had passed when we set sail in a ship which had wintered in the island; she was the Castor and Pollux of Alexandria. We put in at Syracuse and spent three days there; then we sailed round and arrived at Rhegium. After one day a south wind sprang up and we reached Puteoli in two days. There we found fellow Christians and were invited to stay a week with them. And so to Rome. The brothers there had received news of us and came out to meet us as far as Appii Forum and Tres Tabernae. When Paul saw them, he gave thanks to God and took courage.

A Pluralistic Society
Lucian, Alexander or The False Prophet, 38

He established a celebration of mysteries, with torchlight ceremonies and priestly offices, for three days in succession, in perpetuity. On the first day, there was a proclamation, worded as follows and as at Athens: 'If any atheist or Christian or Epicurean has come to spy upon the rites, let him be off, and let those who believe in the god perform the mysteries, under the blessing of Heaven.' Then, at the very outset, there was an 'expulsion', in which he took the lead, saying: 'Out with the Christians,' and the whole multitude chanted in response, 'Out with the Epicureans!'

38

39

ning of the third chapter of his gospel, where he pinpoints the beginning of John's ministry of baptism by listing the ruler of the Roman Empire, the governor of Judea, the regional rulers of Galilee and Ituraea/Trachonitis, together with the prince of Abilene, and for good measure, the ruling high priest and his predecessor who had kept the title. In true historian's fashion of the age, he provides the chronological yardsticks, and, at the same time, he explains to his readers that such a seemingly unimportant event − the baptismal activity of a man named John − is a part of the whole of world history.

Rulers

Tiberius (39) was the emperor during Jesus' ministry. It was his coin Jesus used to explain the necessity of submission to state authority (Mark 12:13-17). It was he who, in AD 26, appointed the prefect Pontius Pilate, who crucified Jesus. We find both Pilate and Tiberius mentioned on a stone inscription found at Caesarea in 1961 (38). This limestone probably belonged to a public building, a "Tiberieum," erected by Pilate in honor of the emperor.

Tiberius has left another trace in Israel. The city of Tiberias was named after him by Herod Antipas, who had it built between AD 17 and 20. In the New Testament, boats from Tiberias arrived near the place where Jesus had fed the five thousand (John 6:23).

Tiberius died in AD 37; by then, Christianity had begun to develop into an active missionary enterprise. Indeed, some of those Roman Christians who had heard Peter's Pentecost address in Jerusalem in AD 30 may have already been meeting as a church in Rome by then. Tiberius had not been particularly friendly to Jews in AD 19; he even expelled them temporarily from Rome. He left the city himself for good in AD 26.

Christianity is an historical religion, firmly rooted in particular times and places. Time and again, Luke highlights this fact by mentioning identifiable names and periods, and time and again, he has been proven correct. One such example is the begin-

Roads

He was able to rule the empire from his retreat on the island of Capri, an example of the effectiveness of Roman communication systems along the roads and seaways. Ships and lighthouses are often depicted in ancient mosaics (40), and some Roman lighthouses remain standing. A particularly impressive one can be seen at Dover, England (41). The trunk roads crossing the Italian peninsula, like the famous Via Appia (42), facilitated travel, too. Someone like Paul, for example, arriving with his Roman guard and other passengers from Syracuse via Rhegium, would have had the choice between continuing by ship along the coast and using the roads toward Rome, or trying a combination of both — a choice mostly determined by weather conditions.

41

With such well-organized links, we can imagine how easy it would have been for the first Christian writers to send their letters and gospels to distant communities and for the recipients to pass them on to others. In favorable conditions, it took a sea mail ship five days to reach Puteoli from Corinth, or a traveler like Cato less than three days to get from North Africa to Rome.

Rival Cults

But it was not only mail or grain, or Christian documents that could travel speedily and efficiently in those days. Many religious and pseudo-religious cults flourished widely, taking root, first of all, in the harbor towns. Interestingly, Paul's ship bore as figurehead the sign of two Greek gods, the *Dioscuri* or "Twin Brothers," Castor and Pollux, sons of Zeus and patrons of seafarers. Superstitious travelers considered it a good "omen" to sail under their constellation, the "Gemini," believed to protect against storm.

Castor and Pollux and their father Zeus belonged to the Greek company of gods, assembled on Mount Olympus (43). Artemis (named Diana by the Romans) is also featured in the New Testament (Acts 19:24-35), and such gods were so popular that even ordinary mortals were named for them. Dionysus, the god of wine and vegetation, often depicted in elaborate mosaics such as this one in Corinth (44), is behind the name of the one Athenian court member who became a Christian after hearing Paul speak (Acts 17:34). Preaching to the assembled philosophers of Athens, Paul had appealed to their search for the "unknown God." Already, many were questioning the existence of the

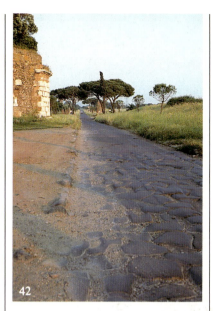

42

traditional gods, though they tended to uphold them as myths essential to their society.

The influence of these deities can still be felt at Cap Sounion in Greece (46), where tourists flock to the temple of Poseidon at dusk, trying to imagine what it must have been like to be an ancient Greek.

In everyday life, many other household gods, old oriental cults, or new-fangled sects shaped people's attitudes. One such example, the Egyptian pair of Isis and Osiris, with their son Horus, even influenced later Christian art. Many Christian depictions of Mary and the Jesus child resemble sculptures of Isis and Horus, with the Christians claiming that the historical virgin birth had finally superseded the old Egyptian myth. Later changed into Serapis, he was widely worshiped. Serapis is referred to in a second-century Christian apologetic writing, the *Octavius* of Minucius Felix, and a second-century statue of him was found as far north as Geneva (45).

With so many godheads to remember and revere, the easiest solution was a temple for "all the gods," a "Pantheon." In Rome, it was duly built in the first century BC and

44

45

reconstructed, after destruction by fire, under Domition in AD 89, and again under Hadrian in AD 110 (48). The Roman Pantheon is thought to be the most perfect single building from antiquity still completely standing. It owes its survival to the fact that its interior (47) was converted into a church in the seventh century. Instead of the old statues of the gods, it now houses memorials and tombs of great Italians, such as the painter Raphael.

In early Christian times, it was easy to come up with a new cult — people were eager to find solace, help, or insurance in "other-worldly" elements. Christians had to compete against such rivals as Alexander, the "false prophet," mocked by the second-century historian and storyteller Lucian of Samosata, who knew him well. And often enough, Christians were lumped together with the hucksters and treated as the despised, superstitious adherents of antisocial movements. Could one expect the ordinary citizen to distinguish between a true revelation and a spurious set-up?

47

48

3. Teaching, Writing, Worshipping

Communicating the Doctrine
Paul, Letter to the Colossians, 4:16-18

Give our greetings to the brothers at Laodicea, and Nympha and the congregation at her house. And when this letter is read among you, see to it that it is also read to the congregation at Laodicea, and that you in return read the one from Laodicea. And tell Archippus: 'Attend to the duty entrusted to you in the Lord's service, and discharge it to the full.'

This greeting is in my, Paul's, own hand. Remember my chains. Grace be with you.

Documenting the Message
Eusebius, Church History 2, 15

Peter's listeners were spiritually enlightened by his preaching — so much so that they were not satisfied with just a single hearing of his teaching. They wanted more than unwritten teaching of God's word, so they persistently sought out Mark, whose gospel is extant and who was Peter's follower. They exhorted Mark to leave them a written statement of the teaching which had been given to them orally. They didn't quit until he was persuaded, which is how we now have the Gospel of Mark.

And they say that Peter, aware of what had been done by the revelation of the Holy Spirit, was pleased at the people's zeal and ratified the scripture for study in the churches. Clement quotes the story in the sixth book of Hypotyposes, and the bishop of Hierapolis, named Papias, confirms him. He also says that Peter mentions Mark in his first Epistle and that he composed this in Rome, which they say that he himself mentions, referring to the city metaphorically as Babylon, in the words, "the elect one in Babylon greets you, and Marcus my son."

Meeting to Learn and Pray
Tertullian, Apology 39:1-3

We are a society with a common religious feeling, unity of discipline, a common bond of hope. We meet in gathering and congregation to approach God in prayer, massing our forces to surround him. This violence that we do him pleases God. We pray also for emperors, for their ministers and those in authority, for the security of the world, for peace on earth, for postponement of the end. We meet to read the books of God — if anything in the nature of the times bids us look to the future or open our eyes to facts. In any case, with those holy words we feed our faith, we lift up our hope, we confirm our confidence; and no less we reinforce our teaching by inculcation of God's precepts.

49

Christians have always regarded Christ as their teacher. We see this portrayed in one of the earliest depictions of Jesus, found at Ostia Antica (50). A fourth-century mosaic preserved in the mausoleum of Santa Constanza in Rome shows Christ giving the new law of the gospel to Peter and Paul (49).

The Teacher's Mantle

Peter and Paul literally took on the teacher's mantle from the Lord. One of the earliest statues of Peter is in fact the statue of a Greek philosopher-teacher, who has been given a new head and a new right hand holding the keys (52); one can still see the marks of the cuts where the new parts were substituted for the old originals. Here, of course, a twofold message was implied. A man like Peter, as the preserver and communicator of Christ's teaching, also assumed the role of the Greco-Roman

50

51

52

IOANNE PAVLO II PONTIFICE MAXIMO
HAEC PERANTIQVA PRINCIPIS
APOSTOLORVM STATVA
QVAM PIVS PP. XII A. MCMXXXXIX RESTAVRAVERAT
HAC IN SEDE AD NOVAM
DIGNIOREMQVE FORMAM REDACTA

philosophers. Their teachings, it was implied, had given way to the true doctrine of the faith.

That formality, that official position of authority, is equally visible in twelfth-century illuminated manuscript (51), where Paul is depicted with an attentive group of recipients of his letters. Paul, in fact, had always been at pains to organize the spread of the faith. Even from prison, he told his readers how to exchange letters and to read them aloud in services.

Early Christian Writing
One of our earliest surviving manuscripts of Paul's letters is the Chester-Beatty-Codex p46 (55), commonly dated about AD 200 but recently shown to be at least 100 years older. Such collections of letters go back to the time when the book-like codex took over from the scrolls, probably in the early 90s of the first century. The oldest known example of a Christian codex has been assumed to be the p52 at the John Rylands University Library of Manchester, England (53), containing John 18:31-33 and 18:37-38. Commonly dated to about AD 125, (but probably a couple of decades older), it may now have been "deplaced" by that collection of Paul's letters, the p46, preserved in two parts at Dublin and Ann Arbor. Scholars are far from unanimous about the actual date of the first Christian writing. Was it a letter of Paul's, or the letter of James, or was it one of the gospels? Recent theories include such early dates as the mid-30s for Matthew or late AD 44 for Mark. It is now certain that the oral tradition was being written down at a much earlier stage than previously assumed. An Early Church author like Clement of Alexandria may well have been correct when he corroborated the tradition that Peter was still alive when Mark's gospel was written and that it was written in Rome. In fact, one controversial papyrus fragment

may be the earliest existing document among these beginnings. It is a tiny part of a scroll, found in Cave 7 at Qumran, and identified by a leading Spanish papyrologist, José O'Callaghan, as Mark 6:52-53 (54). After years

of dispute, scholars are now tending to accept this identification since the Qumran caves were left and sealed in AD 68, and since the handwriting of this particular papyrus argues for a date a couple of decades older still.

— 36 —

This is a very early witness of New Testament writing indeed.

The first Christian writers chose Greek as their language of communication. It was the common language of the eastern parts of the Roman Empire, and even in North Africa or Italy, where Latin was common, Greek was the everyday language of commerce. Above all, it was spoken by the Jews scattered throughout the cities of the empire, who remained the most important single target group during the first six decades of evangelization. From the mid-second century onwards, Latin slowly began to take over, and by AD 180, we know that the gospels and Paul's letters had appeared in Latin, at least in North Africa. Since Latin prevailed in the west and north of the empire, Christian excursions in these directions required a Latin translation of the Bible. Unofficial versions, in what we now call "Itala" or "Old Latin," were used until Pope Damasus instructed the widely traveled priest, Jerome, to translate the whole Bible into Latin afresh on the basis of Old Latin precursors. Jerome accepted and went one step farther: instead of relying on Latin precedents and the Greek texts of the Old and New Testaments, he also consulted the original Hebrew Old Testament. Thus, the result was a Latin version as close to the originals as was possible at the time. He finished his translation in a cave-like monastery cell in Bethlehem in 406, idealized by artists such as Albrecht Dürer in 1512 (56). Called the "Vulgata" (the common one), it was declared the official Bible of the Catholic Church at the Council of Trent in 1546.

The Gathered Believers

In those early days before Jerome Christians did not have churches. When they came together to hear the gospel or one of the apostles' letters,

58

to pray together, and to celebrate the Eucharist, they met in private homes. Some such homes are even mentioned in the New Testament. For example, there is Gaius, whose house was big enough to welcome the whole community of Corinth (Romans 16:23), the house of Aquila and Priscilla (1 Corinthians 16:19), or the upper room at Troas (Acts 20:8), the scene in which one of Paul's listeners, sinking into a deep sleep, fell to the ground from the third floor. Not many of these meeting places have been preserved or rediscovered, but there are a few possible first-century sites. The house underneath the Roman church of Santa Pudenziana (58), according to tradition, is the house of the Pudens mentioned in 2 Timothy 4:21. The house underneath San Clemente (see 112/113) is associated with Clement, a leader in the Roman church and author of an early letter to the Corinthian church. Some say he is the man addressed in Philippians 4:3. The church of Santa Prisca on the Aventine Hill (see 147) has also been associated with New Testament Christians, with the couple of Priscilla (or Prisca) and Aquila, who did have a church meeting in their

59

home (Romans 16:5). First-century living quarters have indeed been found nearby.

A particularly interesting example is preserved underneath the church of Santi Giovanni e Paolo in Rome. Here we have a second-century house on two floors with a central heating system (59) and, behind it, Rome's largest surviving mural, a scene depicting the goddess Venus. Very early, Christians lived in this house, too, but in a different part. People in an attitude of prayer and sleep are portrayed on frescoes, and in one corner, a fourth-century oratory to the memory of the martyrs John and Paul — not the apostles, but second-century Roman civil servants — can be seen.

The catacombs, the burial grounds of Jews and Christians, were also used as meeting places, probably from the late second-century onward. Even in times of persecution, the Christians always knew where to meet, long before the first proper Church was built. But the catacombs were never hiding places. Christians met here to celebrate memorial services for their dead and to share the Eucharist in memory of Christ.

1. A Despised Minority

Be Prepared
Peter, First Letter, 4:12-16

My beloved, do not be bewildered by the fire which is among you as an ordeal, as though it were something extraordinary. It is a cause for joy, for it gives you a share in Christ's sufferings, and when his glory is revealed, your joy will be triumphant. If Christ's name is used against you as an insult, count yourselves happy, because then that glorious Spirit which is the Spirit of God is resting upon you. If you suffer, it must not be for murder, theft, or sorcery, nor for infringing the rights of others. But if anyone suffers as a Christian, he should not be ashamed, but honor God with that name.

A Brutal Diatribe
Minucius Felix: Octavius, 6:1; 8:1-4; 9:1

Why cannot you Christians see the right and better way? You should receive the teaching of our ancestors as if they were the high priests of truth. You should reverence the traditional religion and worship the gods that your parents taught you to fear even before you knew them intimately. You should not pronounce your judgements upon our traditional divinities, but rather you should believe our forefathers. When the world was still uncivilized, when the world was only just born, our forefathers even then showed themselves worthy to receive kindness from the gods and have the gods as their kings! In every empire, province, and city each nationality observes the ritual of its own family and worships its local divinities.

Even though we are sometimes uncertain about the origin of some gods, nevertheless, all peoples are firmly convinced that there are immortal gods, so I can't stand those of you who are so audacious and so swollen with impious pretensions that you are wise, that you think you can try to destroy or weaken our most ancient, useful, and salutary religion. I know that Theodorus of Cyrene, and before him Diagoras of Melos, were called "atheists" by the ancients because both of them asserted that there were no gods. If they had been believed, the fear and veneration by which human behavior is governed would have been utterly destroyed. But their impious doctrines and sham philosophy will never have much influence. Protagoras of Abdera discussed the question of the godhead as a philosopher rather than as an atheist and he was banished by the Athenians and his writings publicly burnt. Excuse me for expressing my intense feelings so freely, but I think it is deplorable that attacks should be made upon the gods, by a gang, yes I mean a gang, of discredited and proscribed desperadoes. This gang (the Christians) has been gathered from the lowest dregs of the population. They are ignorant men and gullible women — and we all know women are naturally unstable. They are a rabble of impious conspirators. At their nighttime meetings, solemn fasts, and barbarous meals, their bond of union is not a sacred rite, but crime. They are a secret tribe that lurks in the darkness and shuts out the light. They are silent in public but chatter in the corners.

Bad weeds grow fast. Their vicious habits spread day by day. Wherever this impious confederacy meets in their abominable haunts they multiply all over the world. These conspirators must be utterly destroyed and cursed!

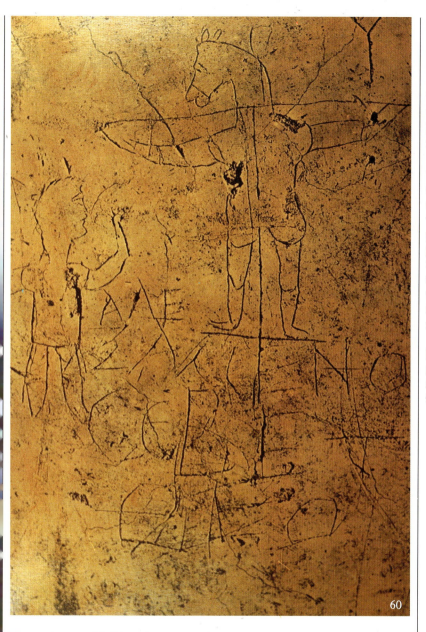

60

assheaded god. The second century authors Minucius Felix (*Octavius* 9:3; 28:7) and Tertullian (*Apology* 16:1-5) knew about this calumny, which had been used against the Jews before it was transferred to the Christians (Tacitus, *Histories* 5,3:2; 4:2; Flavius Josephus, *Against Apion* 2,7:80-81).

This graffito demonstrates at least two things. First, Christians were the subject of public ridicule. But, second, we should note that the graffito was found in the so-called "Paedagogium," the school of the imperial pages on the Palatine. We can infer from this that there was a young boy among them who was a Christian who did not hesitate to confess his faith in an unsympathetic environment, risking ridicule or worse.

The non-Christian citizens of the Roman Empire did not do much to really understand the background of Christianity. It was easier to give in to rumors and handy prejudices.

The modern world did not invent graffiti. Christians were writing on walls as early as AD 79. Examples include the famous acrostic from Pompeii, yielding the Latin words "Our Father" (*Paternoster*) and the symbols of beginning and end, alpha and omega. Of course, Christians were not the only ones to indulge in graffiti. The walls of Pompeii are full of love poems, funny little epigrams, and bawdy comments. We find such irreverent messages even on Rome's Palatine Hill (60). Here, a late second-century Roman mocks a man called Alexameno, because he is praying to a crucified God with the head of an ass. "Alexamenos sebete theon," says the cruel inscription. "Alexamenos prays to (his) God."

It was common at the time to accuse Christians of venerating an

61

62

VETTENACCLA ROD
ECITC VETTENOCL
CHRESTO ET SIBI

63

CHRESTVS
LICTOR·CAESARIS

Appia, not far from the Casal Rotondo (61/62), and again, with the rank of a "lictor" (attendant) of the Caesar, on a stone preserved near the Mausoleum of Cecilia Metella (63).

But Chrestus was not a Jewish name. Thanks to the identical pronunciation of "e" and "i," Suetonius had simply mistaken the name he knew, Chrestus, for the title of Jesus — Christus, the Messiah. So it was probably the message of Christ which had stirred up the Jews against the Christians, as it had done in Jerusalem (Acts 6:9-7:60), Pisidian Antioch (Acts 13:50), or Corinth (Acts 18:12-17). And Claudius, not interested in subtleties, simply expelled Jews and Jewish Christians alike, leaving Suetonius somewhat muddled when he wrote his sentence. Even Tacitus, a more careful historian, who knew that there had been a Christ crucified under Pontius Pilate, uses both "Chrestians" and "Christ" at random in his account of the Neronian persecution (*Annals* 15, 44:3).

The Case of Chrestus

Even in the early second century, the Roman historian Suetonius is at a loss as to how to chronicle the expulsion of the Jews and the Jewish Christians from Rome by the Emperor Claudius in AD 49 (see Acts 18:2). The Jews, he wrote (*Life of Claudius*, 25,4), had assiduously been causing tumults at the instigation of "Chrestus." Chrestus was a fairly common name in Rome; we find it on an inscription at the Via

64

65

Life in the Theater

Christians were living in a pluralistic society. Could they conform to their environment, attending the circus games or the often licentious theater performances or any other form of communal event? Could they risk being despised as outsiders if they abstained and kept apart as the Jews had done for centuries? In the first centuries after Christ, theater in particular had moved away from the austere and purifying tragedy held high by the Greeks and praised by theoreticians such as Aristotle. Seneca, a contemporary of Paul's, wrote his tragedies for the closet, and the stage was being taken over by mimes and pantomimes and by sexually explicit comedies. Masks preserved from those days hint at the spirit behind the texts performed (65). But theaters, like the one at Ostia Antica (64), the ancient harbor of Rome, did play an important part in society, and we may safely assume that even Jesus attended performances at the grandiose theater of Sepphoris, less than four miles from Nazareth, learning about current attitudes and ideas which he was to use in his later ministry. When he called certain doubters "hypocrites," for example, he used the Greek word for "actor." And Paul even quoted from the ribald playwright Menander (1 Corinthians 15:33).

But in the late second century, the influential Christian thinker Tertullian condemned all public spectacles (circus, theater, amphitheater, stadium) as detrimental to the faith. In his diatribe *On the Spectacles*, he called on the Christians to wait for the day of the Last Judgment; then they would witness the greatest spectacle of all, the condemnation of unbelievers (*On the Spectables* 30, 1).

Perhaps one sentence sums up his attitude best. Looking at the often lethal performances in the circus, he asked: "Have you a mind for blood? You have the blood of Christ!" (29:9)

Spectacles apart, keeping oneself aloof was not easy, especially not at the heart of the empire. There, the old legends were held in high regard. The Altar of Peace (*Ara Pacis*), for instance, shows founding father Aeneas sacrificing to the gods (66). And any public debater would have to take Greek philosophy seriously. The Athenian Stoa (67) symbolizes the solid position that Greek ideas had in the minds of Roman thinkers. It took Christians some time to realize that they had to "counter-attack," to follow in Paul's footsteps, to interpret Christianity as providing the superior "spectacle" (without going to the extremes of trying to prohibit all others), and to demonstrate that Christianity was the true fulfillment of philosophy. Justin Martyr, Minucius Felix, and Clement of Alexandria were three of the first Christians to master this art. But for a long time, Christians were regarded by their opponents as those who hid in dark corners, celebrated their "barbarous meals" at nocturnal gatherings in the catacombs (69), scenes smacking of crime and debauchery (68) rather than holy witness. Such was the common misunderstanding of their memorial feasts in the catacombs, a mystery to all those who preferred the supposedly superior light of day which they thought they could find in their own philosophies.

2. Living with Tensions

An Explanation
"Letter to Diognetus," 5:1-17; 6:1-4

For Christians are not distinguished from the rest of mankind by country, or by speech, or by dress. For they do not dwell in cities of their own, or use a different language, or practice a peculiar life. This knowledge of theirs has not been proclaimed by the thought and effort of restless men; they are not champions of a human doctrine, as some men are. But while they dwell in Greek or barbarian cities according as each man's lot has been cast, and follow the customs of the land in clothing and food, and other matters of daily life, yet the condition of citizenship which they exhibit is wonderful, and admittedly strange. They life in countries of their own, but simply as sojourners. They share the life of citizens, they endure the lot of foreigners. Every foreign land is to them a fatherland, and every fatherland a foreign land. They marry like the rest of the world. They breed children, but they do not discard their children as some do. They offer a common table but not a common bed. They exist in the flesh, but they live not after the flesh. They spend their existence upon earth, but their citizenship is in heaven. They obey the established laws, and in their own lives they surpass the laws. They love all men, and are persecuted by all. They are unknown, and they are condemned. They are put to death, and they gain new life. They are poor, and make many rich. They lack everything, and in everything they abound. They are dishonored, and their dishonor becomes their glory. They are reviled, and are justified. They are abused, and they bless. They are insulted, and repay insult with honor. They do good, and are punished as evil-doers; and in their punishment they rejoice as gaining new life therein. The Jews war against them as aliens, and the Greeks persecute them; and they that hate them can state no ground for their enmity.

In a word, what the soul is in the body Christians are in the world. The soul is spread through all the members of the body, and Christians through all the cities of the world. The soul dwells in the body, but it is not of the body. Christians dwell in the world, but they are not of the world.

A Bridge-Building Exercise
Clement of Alexandria, Stromateis, 1, 5, 28:1-3

Philosophy then before the coming of the Lord was necessary to the Greeks to bring them to rightceousness, but now it is profitable to bring them to piety, seeing that it is a sort of training for those who are gaining the fruit of faith for themselves by means of demonstration, for thy foot shall not stumble (Proverbs 3: 23), says he, if you refer good things to providence, whether they be Greek or Christian. For God is the cause of all good things, but of some primarily, as of the old and new covenants, and of others consequentially, as of philosophy. As it happened, it was given primarily to the Greeks in times before the Lord called also the Greeks; for philosophy educated the Greek world as the law did the Hebrews to bring them to Christ (Galatians 3: 24). Philosophy therefore is a preparation, making ready the way for him who is being perfected by Christ.

70

71

72

Take a diverse group of people to-day, say on the Piazza Navona in the center of Rome (71). Looking at them, one would not immediately be able to tell which of them are Christians. Indeed, even supposedly tell-tale signs, like a cross hanging from a chain, are often mere gadgets of fashion. "Professional" Christians, on the other hand, tend to signal their association clearly. Nuns on their way to St Peter's in Rome (72), or a Franciscan in Jerusalem, are imme-diately recognizable, even from afar (70).

In the first centuries, Christians could hardly be distinguished from others by their outfit. The anonymous second-century author of the *Letter to Diognetus* puts it well when he lists what Christians and non-Christians seemingly have in common and where the real differences become obvious, differences which were often mis-interpreted and used against the Chris-tians. Or consider that important dialogue *Octavius* by Minucius Felix. The friends meet again in Ostia after a long time and do not recognize each other's religious allegiances at first

glance. It is only when one of them, Caecilius Natalis, bows to a statue of the god Serapis, which they pass on their way along the shore, that the other two realize that he, unlike them, has not become a Christian. Then the conversation turns to ques-tions of faith. Caecilius starts a long diatribe against the Christians, listing all the gory accusations leveled against them, and Octavius answers with a sober, philosophical analysis of these accusations, refuting them one by one. In this pearl among early Christian literature, Caecilius finally acknowledges defeat, but claims vic-tory nonetheless — for he has over-come his own unbelief.

Tensions among friends and within families were not uncommon. But they did not always end in renewed and deepened friendship, as in the *Octavius*.

73

The Scandal of the Cross

The cross of Christ was elementary to Christian preaching. It is found in Christian art and even on implements of daily life such as lamps for Christian meeting places (73). It was also used in combination with other symbols, like the fish and the anchor, on stones in the catacombs (74). Yet it remained a "scandal" to many. This was not necessarily a failure on the part of the Christians to witness credibly in their private lives. On the contrary, their social and moral tenets, so clearly laid out in the New Testament, were strictly adhered to more often than not. It was the Christians themselves who drew away from their relatives when they were afraid they might compromise their own holiness. Certain passages, like 2 Corinthians 6:14 ("Do not be yoked together with unbelievers") were often taken more literally than others, such as 1 Corinthians 10:27 ("If some unbeliever invites you to a meal and you want to go, eat whatever is put before you without raising questions of conscience") or 1 Corinthians 7:14 ("The unbelieving husband has been sanc-

74

ified through his wife, and the unbelieving wife has been sanctified
through her believing husband.
Otherwise your children would be
unclean, but as it is, they are holy").

75

In many ways, the question of
strictness and absoluteness of Christian doctrines and values in a pluralistic society has become topical
again today. It may therefore be com-
forting to find early examples of
families surviving such tensions and
demonstrating a spirit of uncompro-
mising tolerance even in death. In the
Roman catacombs of San Sebastiano,
we find the family tomb of M. Clodius
Hermes — a name also known from
the New Testament (Romans 16:14).
Next to it, there is a tomb with stucco
on the ceiling, a rose, and in several
niches it is decorated with Christian
inscriptions and symbols. On one of
the entrances, there is a eucharistic
scene. But more importantly, whereas
the non-Christian family members had
been cremated, the Christians had
insisted on internment, so we find
both types of burial virtually next to
each other.

Story in Stone
In Trier, one of the Roman's imperial
seats of government, the sarcophagus
of Albana was discovered in a separate vault in a huge graveyard outside
the ancient city gates (75). Preserved
inside, the bones of a man and a
woman were found, a married couple
portrayed twice on both sides of the
sarcophagus. At one end, a man on
horseback is depicted — the husband,
obviously a high-ranking officer or
civil servant within the Roman administration. But at the other end, we see
the most illuminating element of the
sarcophagus: a meal portraying husband and wife, with the Christian
symbols of bread and fish before
them. Dated about AD 270, three
decades before the terrible persecution under Diocletian, it probably is
the sarcophagus of Albana, who, after
the death of her husband, housed the
first missionary bishops of Trier and
gave away much of her property and
possessions to the local Christian
community. In death, both husband
and wife are shown to be reunited at a
Christian meal.

76

Common Threads

That search for common elements, looking for bridges or building them, was a principle applicable to practically all realms of life. Paul expressed this when he addressed the assembly of the Areopagus in Athens (Acts 17:19-34), a meeting which took place probably not on the Areopagus Hill visited today (78) but at the Royal Stoa where Socrates, too, had been interrogated. The Apostle searched for a common starting point, even if it was nothing more than the realization, often expressed by Greek philosophers, that "we are his (God's) offspring" (Acts 17:28). Tensions will inevitably follow, but there is always the knowledge that thinking people can, if they so wish, return to this common denominator. Athens (76/77), the city of the great philosophical schools, was of vital importance to an educated man like Paul. His initial

78

success was limited, but others followed his example and built on it. In the second century, an Athenian philosopher called Clement became a Christian, traveled to Alexandria in Egypt, and took over a scholarly academy. His surviving writings, among them the *Stromateis* or *Patchwork* and an *Admonition to the Pagans,* are prime examples of this applied Pauline thinking and teaching.

And yet these efforts at philosophical toleration often failed. Clement himself became a victim of society's tensions. During the persecution of Septimius Severus, AD 202/203, he had to flee from Alexandria to Cappadocia in modern Turkey, where he died a decade later.

1. Early Measures, Early Martyrs

A Pagan Testimony:
Rome and the Christians Burning
Tacitus, Annals 15, 44:2-8

All human efforts, the emperor's lavish gifts, and the propitiation of the gods did not banish the sinister belief that the great fire (of Rome) was the result of an order. Consequently, to get rid of that idea, Nero placed the guilt and inflicted bizarre tortures on Christians. The Christians were hated by the general public for their abominations. Christus, the origin of the name "Christians," suffered the extreme penalty, at the hands of one of our procurators, Pontius Pilate, during the reign of Tiberius. Thus a deadly superstition that had been checked for a moment again broke out not only in Judea, where this evil all began, but also in the City (Rome) where all things hideous and shameful from every part of the world meet and become popular. Accordingly, an arrest was first made of all who confessed; then, upon hearing their confessions, an immense multitude was convicted, not so much of arson but of hatred of the human race. Mockery of every sort was added to their deaths. Covered with the skins of beasts, they were torn apart by dogs, nailed to crosses, or doomed to the flames. Those who were burned were used to illumine the night-time skies when daylight ended. Nero had opened his gardens for the spectacle, even exhibiting a show in the circus, while he mingled with the people, dressed as a charioteer or driving in a chariot. Because of this, people felt compassion even for criminals who deserved extreme and exemplary punishment. They realized the Christians were being destroyed, not for the public good but because of Nero's appetite for cruelty.

Enemies Without and Within
Clement of Rome, First Letter to the Corinthians
5:1-7; 6:1-2

Let us come to the athletes of the recent past; let us take the noble examples of our own generation. Through jealousy and envy the greatest and most righteous pillars (of the Church) were persecuted, and contended unto death. Let us set before our eyes the good (i.e. heroic) apostles: Peter, who through unrighteous jealousy endured not one or two but many labors, and so having borne witness proceeded to his due place of glory. Through jealousy and strife Paul displayed the prize of endurance; seven times in bonds, driven into exile, stoned, appearing as a herald in both the East and the West he won noble fame for his faith; he taught righteousness to the whole world, and after reaching the limits of the West, bore witness before the rulers. Then he passed from the world and went to the holy place, having shown himself the greatest pattern of endurance.

Associated with these men of holy life is a great multitude of the elect, who because of jealousy have suffered many indignities and tortures and have set a very noble example in our midst. Because of jealousy women were persecuted, who as Danaids and Dircae suffered terrible and impious indignities and thereby safely completed the race of faith and, though weak in body, received a noble reward of honor.

not mentioned in the New Testament, either. Judging by its historical references, the period covered in Acts obviously ended some time before the great Neronian persecution of AD 64, and years before the destruction of Jerusalem in AD 70. There are a couple of prophetic allusions to Peter's death in John 21:18-19 and 2 Peter 1:13-15, but these are within the limits of what could be said before the event, and it is, of course, quite improbable that the letters or indeed Acts would have omitted the glorious testimonies to the martyrdoms of Peter and Paul, had they happened before these accounts were written.

Early Evidence

Thus, we have to turn to later authors for evidence. Fortunately, we have the testimony of a Roman historian and a Roman Christian who wrote letters.

The historian Tacitus, who lived about AD 55 to AD 116, must have had direct contact with Christians — if not in Rome, then in the Roman province of Asia, where he was proconsul under Emperor Trajan. This "Asia" was not the continent we know today by that name, but a territory within the smaller land mass of "Asia Minor" (modern-day Turkey). Peter's first epistle was addressed to Christians in Asia, as well as other provinces, so we know there was a Christian presence there. We also

Defamation, ridicule, exclusion from office: Christians could live with that. And they could live with the accusation of being parasites, "a class hated for their abominations," as Tacitus wrote. Christians were seen as enemies of the state, the senate, and the people of Rome — the "Senatus Populusque Romanus," SPQR (79). The great apologetic writers like Justin, Irenaeus, Minucius Felix, Tertullian, and others refuted these accusations again and again.

But there was more at stake, quite literally, than such serious examples of social discomfort. The Greek word for "witness" is "martyr," and martyrs were what many of these Christian missionaries and evangelists would soon become. The New Testament tells us of two such martyrs: Stephen (Acts 7:57-60) and James, the brother of John (Acts 12:2). The book of Acts ends before AD 62, the year of the third early martyrdom, that of James, the brother of the Lord, which was recorded by the Jewish historian Flavius Josephus. And the martydroms of the two great pillars of the early church, Peter and Paul, are know of a Christian community in the neighboring province of Bithynia, where Pliny the Younger served as a local governor a few years later. (Pliny wrote to Emperor Trajan about AD 111, wondering how he should deal with the Christians.)

So Tacitus may be reflecting the public image of Christianity in that area when he describes them as "a class hated for their abominations," "a deadly superstition," people convicted of "hatred of the human race," "criminals who deserved extreme and exemplary punishment." But when he reports how Nero (80) used the Christians as scapegoats after the disastrous fire of Rome in July of AD 64, even Tacitus records a certain feeling of compassion among the Romans who found the cruelty of the persecution excessive. After all, it was widely assumed, even by pagan Romans, that Nero himself, not the Christians, had started the fire.

Peter and Paul

Were Peter and Paul among the first victims of Nero's onslaught in AD 64/65? Tradition has it that they were incarcerated in Rome's famous state prison, the Mamertinum (82/83), opposite the Forum. As for Peter, the story goes that he survived the immediate persecution and was advised to leave the city at a later stage to escape the vengeance of husbands whose wives had become Christians. On the Via Appia, outside the city gates, Christ appears to him. Peter asked him: "Lord, where are you going?" Jesus replied that he is going to Rome to be crucified once more. Peter understood, returned to his flock and was duly crucified himself. On the alleged spot of the encounter, the little church of "Domine Quo Vadis" (Latin for "Lord, where are you going?") still stands (81).

HAEIC PETRUS A XSTO PETIIT: DOMINE QUO VADIS

81

This story is told in the late second-century *Acts of Peter*. Whatever one may think of it historically, the fact that Peter died at a later stage and was crucified, head downwards (86), is corroborated by other sources. The most likely time for Peter's martyrdom is the fourteenth year of Nero's reign, between October 14, AD 67, and June 9, AD 68 (the day of Nero's suicide). Peter was buried in a public graveyard near the Neronian circus, on the Vatican Hill, to the west of the city (85). The first church of St Peter was erected here by Emperor Constantine, but all that is left of the supposed site of Peter's martyrdom is the obelisk in the center of St Peter's Square (84), which had been erected at Nero's circus in AD 37 and was moved to its present location in 1586.

Paul, the proud possessor of Roman citizenship, was treated differently. For him, beheading by the sword was the form of death, and there was a special place reserved for such executions, Aquae Salviae (the modern Tre Fontane), to the south of the city. One of the memorial churches erected in this area, which is now in the care of Trappist monks, has the scenes of Peter's and Paul's martyrdoms (86/88) carved in stone. Paul was buried

85

nearby, most likely in AD 67/68 as well, on the Vi
Ostiense. Above his tomb (89), the church o
St Paul Outside the Walls was erected in th
fourth century (87)
Quite frequently, Christians were buried along
side non-Christians in public cemeteries befor
the catacombs came into use. The Vatican grave
yard was one such example, and tombs excavate
underneath St Peter's still show the close proximi
ty of the Christian and non-Christian burials
In the countryside outside Rome, the necro
polis of Ostia Antica (90) provides parti
cularly authentic examples of form
of burial in those days, rangin
from simple tiles in th
ground covering the re
mains, to magnificen
vaults with stucc
and frescoes, wit
ash urns for th
cremated an
sarcophag
for th
interred

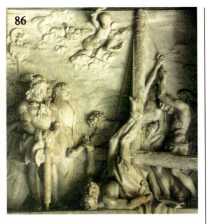

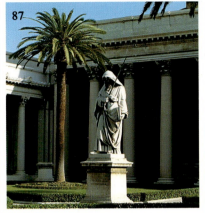

A Different Story

A Christian account of the first Roman persecutions should prevent us from regarding Christians as a perfectly close-knit community, united against a common enemy all the time. There were exceptions. Clement of Rome, in his first letter to the Corinthians, written in the 90s at the latest, but possibly two decades earlier, tells a different story. Jealousy and (internecine) strife were held responsible for the martyrdoms of Peter and Paul and of many others. We are reminded of a sentence in Tacitus's account that Christians were arrested on information supplied by other Christians. Deadly internecine strife was something predicted by Jesus himself long ago (Mark 13:11-13). Here, perhaps, the fire of Rome had given rise to expectations of the end of the world, the beginning of the final conflagration, and to triumphant claims from certain Christians overlooking the smoking ruins. Others, including Peter and Paul, had warned against such premature triumphalism and had thereby incurred the enmity of the zealots for doing so. Clement seems to know of details which he does not reveal. But we gather from what he does say that we should not visualize the early church as an idyllic group of like-minded romantics. And as Paul's own letters, to the Corinthians in particular, unmistakably show, Christians in a pluralistic society have always been prone to the extremes of fanaticism on the one hand or appeasing liberalism on the other and to end up fighting each other over the definition of true faith. The witness of martyrs to the unadulterated message of Jesus therefore serves as a salutary reminder of Christian credibility to the "outside" world.

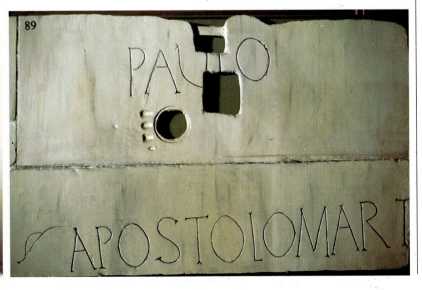

2. Fragile Relief

"Simple Folk"
Hegesippus, Recollections, in:
Eusebius, Church History 3, 20:1-6

Two grandsons of Judas (supposed brother of Jesus and of the family line of David) were still living. The officer brought these men to Domitian Caesar because, like Herod, he was afraid of Christ's coming. Caesar asked them if they were of the house of David, and they admitted it. Then he asked them how much property and money they controlled. They said they only possessed nine thousand denarii between them, half belonging to each. They stated that they didn't possess this amount in money, however. It was instead the value of the thirty-nine plethra of land on which they lived and paid taxes and for which they had to work. The men then showed them their hands, illustrating their labor and the hardness of their bodies. The men were then asked about Christ and his kingdom, its nature, origin, and time of appearance. They explained that it was neither earthly nor of the world but heavenly and angelic. They said it would appear at the end of the world when Christ would come in glory to judge the living and the dead and to reward all people according to their deeds. Hearing this, Domitian did not condemn them but wrote them off as simple folk and released them. He then decreed an end to the persecution against the Church. When the men were released, they became the leaders of the churches, both for their testimony and their relation to the Lord. They shared the gospel and remained alive in the peace which ensued until Trajan.

Legal Enlightenment
Trajan, Letter to Pliny, in:
Pliny the Younger, Letters, 10, 97

You have adopted the proper course, my dear Secundus, in examining the cases of those who were accused of being Christians. Indeed, nothing can be laid down as a general ruling involving something like a set form of procedure. Christians are not to be sought out; but if they are accused and convicted, they must be punished. But, note this condition: If someone denies being a Christian and is able to prove he isn't by worshipping our gods, he shall be pardoned. His change of mind shall be accepted no matter how suspicious his past conduct may be. Do not, however, accept any anonymous charges or unsigned papers as evidence against them, for they are a very bad example and a waste of our time.

Even-handed Justice
Hadrian, Rescript to Proconsul
C. M. Fundanus, in:
Eusebius, Church History 4, 9

If our subjects in the provinces are able to provide evidence against the Christians before a Court of Justice, I have no objection. But I do not allow them to use mere clamorous demands and outcries for this purpose. For it is much more fair, if anyone wishes to accuse them, for you to take cognizance of the matters laid to their charge. Thus, if anyone accuses the Christians and can prove that they were acting contrary to the laws, then determine their punishments in accordance with their offenses. You must be very carefully aware though, I say by Hercules, of people accusing Christians just for the sake of sullying their names. If this happens, proceed against the accusers with heavier penalties because of their heinous guilt.

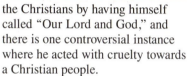

Not all rulers were interested in persecuting all the Christians all the time. Following road signs in Rome today (91), one is soon led to the Piazza Navona, the former circus of Emperor Domitian (92). In fact, the oval shape of the circus is still clearly marked by the buildings surrounding the piazza. At the northern end, excavations have yielded one of the entrance gates to the old circus, and to the left, there is the church of St Agnes in Agone with its ancient crypt, preserving the memory of a martyr saint executed later on this spot. But was Domitian himself really a great persecutor? Can he really be credited with a cruelty and efficiency that nearly destroyed the Christian community at the end of his 15-year reign (AD 81-98)? Some interpreters of the last book of the New Testament, Revelation, have seen him as the evil "eighth emperor," and that book has therefore often been dated to the period of his reign or soon after.

But even Tertullian, who once likened him to Nero, had to admit that the Emperor gave up his attempt at organized persecution very soon. It is true that he did not endear himself to

the Christians by having himself called "Our Lord and God," and there is one controversial instance where he acted with cruelty towards a Christian people.

The Clemens Scandal

The consul Flavius Clemens (a cousin of Domitian) and his wife Domitilla were Christians. They were persecuted on a charge of "atheism, for which many others, who had drifted into Jewish ways, were also condemned," as the second/third century pagan historian Dio Cassius put it (*History* 67,14). Tradition has it that the "Jewish ways" were in fact a reference to Christianity, still seen by many as a Jewish offshoot, and that the couple may have refused to give their allegiance to any other "Lord and God" than Jesus Christ. Since Domitian had designated their two sons his heirs, the matter would have been a political sensation. Clemens was executed, and Domitilla was sent into exile in AD 95. Her steward, Stephanus, organized a conspiracy against Domitian which led to his assassination in AD 96. When the family property was subsequently restored to her, Domitilla gave parts

of her lands to the Christian community. The huge Domitilla catacombs at the Via Ardeatina are situated on family property, and inscriptions of tombs bear the names of members of her family. A crypt discovered there belonged to the family of the Acilii Glabriones. It was an Acilius Glabrio who had been executed with Flavius Clemens on the same charge.

Domitian had no sympathy for the Jews either — he exacted a high Jewish tax and forbade any conversions to Judaism in Rome. As for Jewish Christians, the second-century author Hegesippus tells a fascinating little story, quoted here, at the beginning of the chapter. Domitian interrogated two grandsons of Jude, the brother of Jesus, because he was afraid that their family's claim, that they belonged to the Royal House of David, might cause political trouble. But they were released as soon as Domitian realized that the message of the gospel was no threat to his earthly rule. Obviously, he did not understand the theological implications of their reply, but at least he proved to be a discriminating anti-Christian, not a totalitarian persecutor bent on annihilation.

93

94

95

A Moderate Opponent

Trajan (95), who became Emperor after Domitian's successor Nerva in AD 98, was less paranoid and more enlightened than any of his predecessors. His legacy includes a number of buildings all over the empire, such as at Xanten in northwest Germany, the former Colonia Ulpia Traiana (94) or in Rome, where his markets remain impressive examples of Roman housing construction (93). A correspondence between him and his legate in Pontus and Bithynia, the younger Pliny, has also survived.

Pliny's provinces had been Christianized at least since the period immediately preceding Peter's first letter (see 1 Peter 1:1). In AD 111, the insecure governor writes to his emperor, telling him of his methods used against the Christians, including interrogation, torture, and execution. Yet he wondered if there were any imperial regulations against this "perverse superstition" which proved to be so "contagious." Trajan's reply, quoted at the beginning of this chapter, is an example of moderate ruling — moderate, that is, from the point of view of someone bound to protect his empire against any form of civil unrest. He would have good reasons to fear secret societies or clubs, and the Church was often regarded as such. Still, Trajan made clear that random persecution was impermissible and that no arrests should be made solely on the basis of anonymous tips.

The most famous martyr of that period was Ignatius, Bishop of Antioch, who was sent to Rome and executed in AD 107 or 109. On his journey from Syria to Rome, he wrote seven surviving letters, the most important early documents detailing the Christian attitude towards martyrdom. And Symeon, the successor of James, as leader of the community in Jerusalem, is also said to have died a martyr's death under Trajan. This may have occurred during one of the Jewish revolts against the Romans in AD 115, when Jews and Jewish Christians were lumped together once more.

Hadrian

Trajan's successor as emperor, Hadrian, has been extolled by historians and poets ever since his own time. A poet himself (enjoying homosexual innuendos), he is very much visually alive, thanks to a number of magnificent buildings which have survived. The Castel Sant' Angelo, still crowning the sykline of Rome (97), was

97

built between AD 125 and 139 as a mausoleum for Hadrian and his successors. It was later turned into a church, a fortress, and, today, a museum. At least as impressive is Hadria's villa at Tivoli outside Rome, the largest complex of buildings and landscape developed by one man and surviving from antiquity. The statues placed between the columns of the "Canopo" (98) represented heroes and gods, among them the Hercules mentioned in Hadrian's rescript to Minucius Fundanus, the proconsul of Asia, in AD 124. One reads the text quoted here, at the beginning of the chapter, as a model of careful imperial policies, following Trajan's example. But, like Trajan, Hadrian did not protect the Christians as such. He protected citizens against unlawful accusation. If properly convicted, Christians still had to be prosecuted.

98

3. Turning the Screw

Dying for the Faith
The Martyrdom of Polycarp, 13:2-14:3

They surrounded Polycarp with all of the materials for the burning. When they were ready to fasten him by nails, he said: "Let me be as I am. I don't need to be nailed. He who grants me power to endure the fire will enable me to stand fast unflinching in the fire without being fastened."

So they did not nail him, but they did bind his hands behind his back as if he were a choice ram selected to be offered as a sacrifice — like a whole burnt offering made ready and acceptable to God.

Then Polycarp looked up to heaven and said: "O Lord God Almighty, Father of thy beloved and blessed child Jesus Christ, through whom we have received our knowledge of thee, God of Angels and Powers and of all creation and of the whole race of the righteous who live before thy face, I bless thee in that thou hast deemed me worthy of this day and hour; that I might take a portion among the martyrs in the cup of Christ, to the resurrection of eternal life both of soul and body."

Letter of the Churches in Lyons and Vienne, in: Eusebius, Church History 5, 1:3-63 (here: 50-56)

The crowd was enraged at those who had at first denied they were Christians and were now confessing their Christianity. The people cried out particularly against Alexander, blaming him. Therefore, the governor summoned him and asked him who he was. He replied, "A Christian." This angered the governor; he condemned Alexander to the wild beasts.

The next day, Alexander and Attalus entered the amphitheater together. Attalus had also been thrown to the wild beasts by the governor in order to please the crowd. These men experienced every kind of torture that has been devised for the amphitheater and, in the end, after mighty conflict, they were sacrificed like the ones before. Alexander neither groaned nor uttered the slightest cry but instead prayed in his heart to God. Attalus, however, addressed the multitude in Latin as he was placed in the iron chair and scorched, fumes rising from his body. He said: "Behold, this which you do is devouring men; but we neither devour men nor practice any other wickedness."

Later, on the last day of the single combats, Blandina was again brought in along with Ponticus, a boy of about fifteen. They had been brought in every day previously to view the tortures of the others. The heathen tried to force them to swear by their idols, but the two remained firm. This only infuriated the crowd. It had neither compassion for the youth of the boy nor respect for the sex of the woman. Instead, the crowd exposed them to every cruelty and forced them to experience the entire round of tortures. They did this over and over, trying to get them to deny their faith. It was unsuccessful, however. Ponticus, encouraged by his sister (even the heathen saw that she was urging him on and strengthening him), gave up his spirit after having endured every kind of torture.

But the blessed Blandina last of all, having, like a high-born mother, exhorted her children and sent them forth victorious to the King, travelled the same painful path as they did and hastened to them rejoicing and exulting at her departure as one hidden in a marriage supper rather than cast to the wild beasts. After all of the tortures — scourging, wild beasts, the frying pan — she was at last thrown into a basket and presented to a bull. The animal tossed her for a while, but she had lost all perception of what was happening to her because she had hope, faith, and a personal relationship with Christ. Finally, she was sacrificed. Even the heathen acknowledged that never in their experience had a woman endured so many terrible sufferings.

Persecutions could happen in different ways. But hardly ever did they affect the whole empire simultaneously. Most of them were regional or local. When Nero persecuted the Christians after the fire of Rome, even he may have confined this measure to the city. But we hear about a so-called "Institutum Neronianum," mentioned by Tertullian in AD 197 (*To the Nations* 1,7:9). He implies that this "institutionalized" persecu-

tion was empire-wide and even outlasted the end of Nero's reign. The non-Christian historian Suetonius, writing several decades earlier, also seems to know of more than just a little local incident (*Life of Nero*, 6,16:2). Whatever may have happened, legates, procurators, or prefects all over the empire were likely to follow the capital's example even if not expressly ordered to do so. In any case, there was a certain entertainment

value for the populace in a proper persecution. Thus, these happenings were celebrated publicly, in the circuses, the gardens, the amphitheaters. Rome itself had plenty of them, like the enormous Circus Maximus, which dated back to 329 BC. It was 650 yards long, with a width of more that 160 yards. Its empty shell still fills a wide field to the northeast of the Palatine Hill. On a model of fourth-century Rome (99), it is clearly

100

101

102

visible not far from another colossal structure, the Colosseum (properly called the Amphitheatrum Flavium), which was begun by Vespasian in AD 70 and finished under Titus in AD 80. In later public imagination, this colosseum (100) was always remembered as the focal point of persecutions in Rome. In 1749, the arena (101) was even dedicated to the memory of the Christian martyrs, and a giant cross, which has since been removed to one of the old entrances, was placed in the center. Fifty thousand spectators could easily attend a performance here. Overlooking the Forum Romanum from the Palatine Hill (102), one sees the colosseum behind the Arch of Titus, two symbols of persecution, the latter against the Jews, the former against the Christians.

103

104

renounce his faith and was condemned to die by fire. His words to his tormentors and the onlookers were faithfully recorded by surviving Christians. Outside of Scripture, this story is the oldest account of a Christian martyrdom. It was sent to the church of Philomelium, east of Ephesus, in modern Turkey. Even the short extract quoted here at the beginning of the chapter reveals the strength of Polycarp's witness and the clarity of his testimony.

Lyons and Vienne
One of Polycarp's students, a bishop named Irenaeus, played a role in the transmission of another such report a couple of decades later. Newly appointed bishop of Lyons in Gaul (modern France) in AD 178, Irenaeus carried a letter to Rome reporting the horrendous execution of Christians in Lyons and Vienne. He later became known for his theological writings against church heresies.

The letter that he carried from the churches in Lyons and Vienne, however, is anything but a theoretical treatise. It is the gory, moving, authentic account of the martyrdom of countless Christians, male and female, old and young, in the Amphitheater of Lyons (104) in AD 177/178. The young girl Blandina, referred to at the end of the selection that begins this chapter, became one of the most remembered and beloved martyrs in all of Christian history. She was the last to die in the Lyons-Vienne persecution. The letter to the churches explained how she had strengthened and encouraged those who died before her and "like a high-born mother exhorted her children and sent them forth victorious to the King." Then the specifics of the treatment of Blandina herself are given in chilling graphic detail. Finally, she was sacrificed. The letter records that later even the heathen confessed that they had never seen a woman endure

The Aged Bishop
Many regional persecutions were caused, not by any actual decree from a governor, but by a rabble-rousing mob who held the Christians responsible for every ill in society — just as "alien" minorities are often treated today, with the local ruler giving in to popular demand. The martyrdom of Polycarp about AD 155 is a case in point. Polycarp was an influential theologian, bishop of Smyrna (103), modern Izmir in Turkey, an opponent of heretics, trusted interlocutor of men like Ignatius and Irenaeus, letter

writer, and negotiator. One by one, Christians at Smyrna had been tortured, slowly brought to death by all sorts of ingenious implements, neatly detailed in a contemporary account, the *Martyrdom of Polycarp,* written about AD 156. Eventually, a young man called Germanicus had been forced to fight with wild beasts (105), and once he was dead, the mob demanded the life of the leader of the community, the octogenarian Polycarp, who had just returned from Rome.

Polycarp courageously refused to

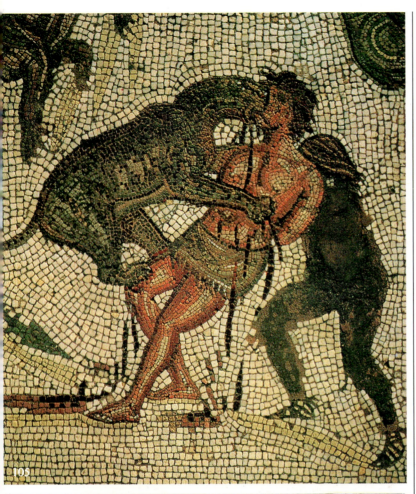

such cruel and prolonged torment.

Blandina and her colleagues are memorialized by a stone at the place of their martyrdom in the amphitheater at Lyons (106). Fellow-believers who were witnesses to the martyrdoms reported that often, as they saw the brothers and sisters in their sufferings, they saw Christ.

The Philosopher Emperor

Interestingly, the Roman emperor at the time was Marcus Aurelius, whose teacher had been the fervently anti-Christian rhetorician Fronto. We think of him as a philosopher-emperor, as the author of a Stoic book of reflections called "To himself." But unlike that earlier great Roman Stoic, Seneca, Marcus Aurelius did not have much in common with Christian moral and ethical thinking. He thought little of what he knew about Christianity, and never (as far as we know) reacted to the learned apologetic writings sent and dedicated to him by Melito of Sardis or Justin Martyr. And the fact that this Justin was martyred in Rome about AD 165 — under the eyes, as it were, of Marcus Aurelius — reminds us of the limitations of this supposedly enlightened, philosophical emperor. Ironically, Justin had been one of the first to introduce Greco-Roman philosophical thinking into the explanation of the Christian faith.

Wherever we look in the mid- and late second century, we find proof of a tightening of the screw. Arguments do not matter, tolerance has become scanty, mob rule has become rife, and the Christians gain strength in martyrdom. Small wonder then that among the most widely distributed early Christian writings are such accounts of martyrdoms sent abroad soon after the events.

1. A Growing Number of Witnesses

Bitter Irony
Tertullian, Apology 40, 2

No matter what happens − if the Tiber reaches the walls, if the Nile does not rise to the fields, if the sky doesn't move or the earth does move, if there is famine, or if there is plague, the cry is at once: "The Christians to the lion!" What does this mean − all of them to one lion?

Following Christ in Martyrdom
Letter of the Churches
in Lyon and Vienne, in Eusebius,
Church History, 5, 2:3-4

They gladly conceded the title of martyr to Christ, the faithful and true martyr and firstborn of the dead and originator of divine life, and they referred to the martyrs now departed, and said: "They are now martyrs, whom Christ deemed worthy to be taken up in their confession, setting upon them the seal of martyrdom by their departure; but we are ordinary and lowly confessors." And with tears they implored and asked the brethren for their earnest prayers that they might be perfected. And although they showed the power of martyrdom in their actions, using great boldness towards the heathen, and manifested their heroism by endurance, fearlessness, and dauntlessness, they were filled with the fear of God and refused to be called martyrs by their brethren.

The Last Great Onslaught
Eusebius, on Diocletian's first Edict, in
Church History 8, 2:4-5

It was the nineteenth year of the reign of Diocletian, and the month Dystrus, or March, as the Romans would call it, in which, as the festival of the Savior's Passion was coming on, an imperial letter was everywhere promulgated, ordering the razing of the churches to the ground and the destruction by fire of the Scriptures, and proclaiming that those who held high positions would lose all civil rights, while those in households, if they persisted in their profession of Christianity, would be deprived of their liberty. Such was the first document against us. But not long afterwards we were further visited with other letters, and in them the order was given that the presidents of the churches should all, in every place, be first committed to prison, and then afterwards compelled by every kind of device to sacrifice.

The martyrs of Lyons and Vienne were remembered in later art (107) as well as in remnants such as the prison cell of Pothinus (108), who preceded Irenaeus as bishop of Lyons. Their sheer courage and endurance outweighed their human fear and weakness. Above all, they knew and openly declared that they were not trailblazers but followers. "They gladly conceded the title of martyr to Christ, the faithful and true martyr and firstborn of the dead and Prince of the life of God," as the Letter of the Churches of Lyons and Vienne puts it. They had Paul in mind, whose message was unequivocal: "We are hard pressed on every side, but not crushed; perplexed, but not in despair; persecuted, but not abandoned; struck down, but not destroyed. We always carry around in our body the death of Jesus, so that the life of Jesus may also be revealed in our body. For we who are alive are always being given over to death for Jesus' sake, so that his life may be revealed in our mortal body (2 Corinthians 4:8-11). And Peter, in his first letter (4:12-13): "Dear friends, do not be surprised at the painful trial you are suffering, as though something strange were happening to you. But rejoice that you participate in the sufferings of Christ, so that you may be overjoyed when his glory is revealed."

Again, we must not forget that these people were real, historical figures, unlike some later martyr saints of obscure provenance whose existence and fate may sometimes have been invented or embellished for the sake of edification and meditation. One such example is St George, the patron saint of England. He may indeed have existed and been martyred in Lydda, Israel, about AD 303, but none of the stories told about him — the fight with the dragon or his voyage to England via the Irish Sea ("St George's Channel") for instance — are anything more than legends. But with the earliest accounts of martyrs — Justin, Ignatius, Polycarp, the believers of Lyons and Vienne and of Scilli in North Africa, or Cyprian, bishop of Carthage — we are on solid ground. A few of the later versions have added questionable details, but the original texts of these stories stand up well to historical perusal. Very early, the church began to collect these martyrdom reports and read them for encouragement in tough times. The story of the martyrs Perpetua and Felicitas, who died AD 202/203 in Carthage, was especially influential, since part of the account consists of notes from Perpetua herself.

Their story may have been compiled by Tertullian, a noted lawyer-turned-theologian of the early church. In his writings, Tertullian occasionally reflects on persecutions with bitter irony. "The Christians to the Lion! What, all of them to one Lion?" Indeed, lions enough there were, but to the Christians, they also represented a kind of eschatological hope — a hope reflected in catacomb carvings (109) and based on prophesies like Isaiah 11:6-7: "The wolf will live with the lamb, the leopard will lie down with the goat, and the calf and the lion and the yearling together; and a little child will lead them. The cow will feed with the bear, their young will lie down together, and the lion will eat straw like the ox."

Worshiping the Gods

What could Christians do to avoid being persecuted? Let us suppose for a moment that they managed to convince the authorities that their faith had been founded on a man unjustly crucified under Roman authority as a dangerous rebel back in Jerusalem. Let's say they would succeed in proving that they did not indulge in drinking blood and eating flesh at nocturnal gatherings, and that they were generally obedient to the state authority anyway. They would still fall afoul of one of the elementary tenets of the empire: The gods had to be revered, and, at least since Domitian, the emperor himself had to be venerated as a deity.

It was Emperor Decius (AD 244-251) who, along with his devastating, empire-wide persecution, introduced the *libelli*, certificates proving that a person had made sacrifice to the gods (110). Only those who had such a *libellus* were safe; those who refused to obtain one could be imprisoned and executed. Many Christians succumbed to the pressure, sacrificed and signed a *libellus* in the presence of witnesses. Others bribed the authorities and were granted a *libellus* in this way. In the example reproduced here, one of 43 found in Egypt and all dated between June 12 and July 14, 250, a certain Hermas, not used to writing, signed his name in big capital letters (line 15).

The Great Persecution

The persecution under Decius was not the last. Even more devastating and nearly successful in eliminating Christians from society was the one instituted by Diocletian, who ruled from 284 to 305. On February 23, 303, he began a persecution which was to continue more or less unabated until 311, even after his abdication and self-imposed exile at Salona (in modern Yugoslavia). It may be an

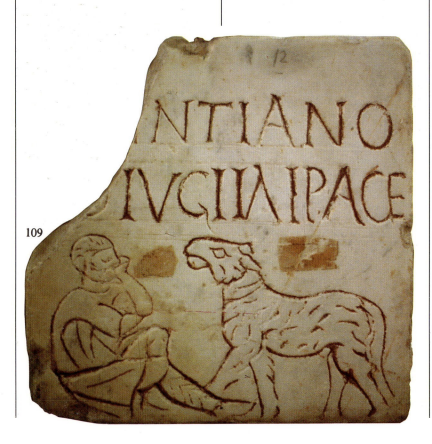

109

110

111

new churches and the copying of Bibles from surviving manuscripts.

Whereas Christian art in those decades refrained from depicting the sufferings and the crucifixion of Jesus, we find many late second — and early third-century scenes on sarcophagi, showing "the first of the apostles," Peter, being led away to his martyrdom in Rome (111), reflecting the prophecy of Jesus in John 21:18-19.

Again and again, the church found solace and strength in the example of the very first Christians. And they remained loyal to to their local roots. Often the authorities would take away their house churches and put them to another use, such as at San Clemente

irony of history (or perhaps a sign of God's subtle sense of justice) that Diocletian died only months after the final victory of Christianity (the Edict of Milan, February 313), powerless to prevent it.

The account of Eusebius, printed here in part at the beginning of this chapter, reveals the havoc wrought by Diocletian, and not only through the countless martyrdoms. The destruction of the churches, and, more importantly, of the many papyri and codices with biblical writings, was devastating. One of the first things Constantine had to organize a few years later, when he finally made Christianity legal, was the building of

114

112

113

in Rome. We know that Christians had been there since the mid-first-century — a first-century alleyway (112), rooms, and a small statue of the Good Shepherd (113) have been found there — corroborating written tradition. Although these Christians were evicted and had to let followers of the cult of Mithras take over the property (114), they were later to return and build an impressive church on the very spot. And they and others in a similar position were encouraged to do so by Constantine and his successors.

2. Building the Church against the Odds

Heretics and Gnostics
Tertullian, On Measures Against the Heretics, 37

Thus, not being Christians, they have acquired no right to the Christian Scriptures; and it may be very fairly said to them, "Who are you? When and whence do you come? As you are none of mine, what are you doing on my property? Indeed, Marcion, by what right do you hew my wood?
By whose permission, Valentinus, are you diverting my streams? By what power, Apelles, are you removing my landmarks? This is my property. Why are you, the rest, sowing and pasturing here at your pleasure? This is my property. I have long possessed it; I possessed it before you. I hold sure title-deeds from the original owners themselves, to whom the estate belonged. I am the heir of the apostles. Just as they disposed of it by their will, and committed it to a trust, and adjured the trustees, even so do I hold it. As for you, they have, it is certain, always held you as disinherited, and rejected you as outsiders, as enemies.

Tertullian, Against the Valentinians, 7

They turned that edifice which is the world into an enormous apartment block, which rises to the sky with as many stories as the skyscraper of the Felicula in Rome. And under its highest roofing tiles, they place God.

Lapsed Christians
Dionysius of Alexandria,
Letter to Fabius, Bishop of Antioch, in:
Eusebius, Church History 4,41:9-12

Immediately, the news spread abroad. The rule that had been more kind to us was changing; now the fear of threatened punishment hung over us. What is more, the edict arrived; it was almost like that which the Lord predicted. It was most terrible so as to cause, if possible, even the elect to stumble. All cowered with fear. A number of the more eminent persons came forward immediately through fear. Others, because of their business in public positions, were compelled to come forward. Others were dragged forward by those around them. Each of these was called forward by name. They approached the impure and unholy sacrifices, some pale and trembling, as if they were themselves the sacrifices and victims to the idols. The large crowd that stood around heaped mockery upon them. It was evident that they were by nature cowards in everything — cowards both to die and to sacrifice. Others, however, ran eagerly toward the altars, affirming by their forwardness that they had never been Christians. For these, the Lord truly predicted that they shall hardly be saved.

Origen, Against Celsus 3,51

But Christians mourn as dead men those who have been overcome by licentiousness or some outrageous sin because they have perished and died to God. They admit them some time later as though they had risen from the dead provided that they show a real conversion, though their period of probation is longer than that required of those who are joining the community for the first time. But they do not select those who have fallen after their conversion to Christianity for any office or administration in the Church of God, as it is called.

116

During the first centuries, church-building was not so much an architectural as a theological task. All over the empire, deviations from the origi-

nal message of faith threatened the inner development of the communities. The New Testament already provides early examples: Paul's two letters to the Corinthians were written in part to counter such deviations. Second Peter, Jude, and certain passages in Revelation also speak out against "heresies" (from the Greek word for something picked out of the whole). Many of these teachings came from the East, but they soon established themselves in Rome itself in the densely built-up quarters of the city, mainly along the river (115).

Tertullian, in a writing directed against one of these sects, the Valentinians, likens their worldview to something like a skyscraper, where God is placed under the highest roofing tiles. The tall building he had in mind was the tenement house of the "Felicula," about 70 feet high, singled out by Roman writers as an

architectural abnormality. This particular house has not survived, but the five surviving stories of the house near the church of Santa Maria in Aracoeli (116) suggest what a complete building of that type would have looked like. In fact, modern inner-city high-rise apartments are probably no great advance on such Roman housing.

A Special Knowledge?
These Valentinians were named after their founder, a certain Valentinian, who was active in Rome about AD 135 and continued to influence his adherents for decades via letters, homilies, and self-composed psalms. He was one of those who practiced what has come to be known as Gnosticism (from *gnosis*, a Greek word meaning "knowledge"). What Gnosticism really was is still hotly disputed among modern scholars. Even con-

117

118

world (119) were all the more insidious because of their constant use of biblical concepts, quotations, or allusions.

Marcion's "Purity"

Another kind of heresy which had to be fought in the process of church building was represented by Marcion. A member of the church in Rome between AD 140 and 144, he was excommunicated for his teaching. He had taught that there were two types of God — the cruel creator who ruled his failed creation by iron laws of retaliation and the God of mercy, revealed by Jesus, and thus unknown before Jesus. This merciful God remained alien to this world because his unlimited love would not be understood by a world full of hatred. Consequently, Marcion tried to "expurgate" from the Bible all those writings which contradicted his theology. Tertullian declared his harsh verdict, quoted at the beginning of this chapter, against the way Marcion and other heretics meddled with Scripture. Marcion's case was special in that he even published his own "canon," with a "purified" collection of Paul's letters, and only one gospel,

temporaries were uncertain and wrote conflicting accounts and rebuttals. Since the discovery of manuscripts at Nag Hammadi in Upper Egypt, in 1946, we have a slightly clearer idea of what gnostic theology looked like. It reinterpreted the meaning of the basic sacraments (baptism, eucharist, last rites), and substituted secret mystery rites for parts of those sacraments. Gnostics refused to accept the authority of orthodox bishops or church institutions as such and speculated freely about creation, cosmology, or the end of the world. They invented a new type of creator-god and a new savior-god of light who opposed the god of darkness.

Such concepts changed the true Christian faith beyond recognition. Gnostic writings such as the "Text without Title" on the origin of the

119

that of Luke, also "purified." It may well be that the late second-century catacomb fresco, showing Paul with a container of five scrolls at his feet (117), is a counter against Marcion's surgical efforts. Here we have the fullness of the historical writings of the church – the four gospels and Acts, the second part of Luke's gospel.

Light and Dark

Sects and heresies that tried to use Christian elements for their own purposes were widespread. Among these were the Manichaeans, named after the Persian Mani, who died in AD 277. Their influence even reached Augustine, one of the great "fathers of the church," who attended their gatherings for almost ten years before he saw through their pseudo-Christian attire and opposed them. Mani, too, had developed a form of "dualism," dividing the universe into the realm of the God of Light and that of the Un-God of Darkness, two realms

which were totally unconnected at the beginning and will be so again at the end of time. In the interim – i.e. in our world-time – the two realms were mixed to detrimental effect, and it was the adherents of the good realm who were suffering. Such a "theology" was attractive in times of crisis. In spite of state and church condemnations, Manichaeism continued to thrive until the Middle Ages. A tenth-century illuminated manuscript (118) shows their legacy in East Turkistan (in modern China). The twelfth-century Cathares, or Albigensians, centered in Southern France, also showed signs of Manichaean influence and were virtually eliminated by an inner-Christian crusade, the so-called Albigensian Wars, between 1208 and 1229.

And there were others: "Docetism" (teaching that Christ had only appeared to be united with the human being Jesus of Nazareth, but had not in reality done so, so that the true Christ did not suffer on the cross) –

a teaching refuted as early as John's first letter (1 John 4:1-3) in the New Testament; or "antinomianism" (teaching that by faith and the free gift of God's grace Christians freed from any obligation to follow moral law, that whatever one did was of no consequence to one's spiritual well-being) – a teaching attacked head on in the short New Testament letter of Jude; or teachings which involved the distortion of Jewish tradition, under the influence of Essene elements (and attacked more than once by Paul, and in Peter's second letter). The examples are countless, extending from the controversies which confronted New Testament letter writers on to the time of Constantine and beyond to the present day.

It was Paul who recognized that things would not improve after his own time. "For the time will come," he wrote in 2 Timothy 4:3-5, "when men will not put up with sound doctrine. Instead, to suit their own desires, they will gather around them a great number of teachers to say what their itching ears want to hear. They will turn their ears away from the truth and turn aside to myths."

121

120

The Lapsed

The church faced a different problem with those who left the church under pressure, sacrificing to the pagan gods to avoid persecution but then repenting and seeking to return. Should they be allowed to support and build the church? At Carthage, Bishop Cyprian tried to settle the question after the Decian persecution. The apostates would be allowed to do penance, but they would not be allowed back into the church. Only clergy could be readmitted, in the face of death, but they would not be allowed to resume office.

Cornelius, pope in Rome from 251, very much followed the same prin-ciples, and, as a result, found himself with an anti-pope, Novatian — a leading theologian and author of a brillant book on the Trinity which has survived. Novatian thought that the church was a spiritual elite and that none who had ever left this group, for whatever reason and under whatever pressure, could be readmitted. In the end, the view of Cornelius and men like Cyprian was to prevail. They saw the church as a mixture of the spiritually advanced and of ordinary, unprivileged people who should be given the chance to do penance and, under certain circumstances, even to be readmitted into the community of Christian brothers and sisters.

The conflict became an issue again after the persecution of Diocletian, and again, the reactions were different. Once more, the successors of Novatian elected an anti-pope, and again the more "warm-hearted" position prevailed. In North Africa, Donatus taught that someone who had handed over the Scriptures to a persecutor was guilty of a crime so severe that anyone who even talked or met with him was equally guilty of the crime and had to be treated as an apostate, too. The Donatist movement split from Rome and effectively established a rival church which was dissolved only in the late fourth century.

123

Building Churches

One of the consequences of such conflicts was the definition given to the sacraments by the orthodox church. The church maintained that the sacrament is and remains valid irrespective of the moral integrity of those who administer it.

Despite such internal Christian struggles, often stemming from the external persecutions, Christians used their occasional periods of calm to establish house churches, assembly rooms, and even some church buildings. These churches were built as much against the odds as the Christian church as a whole. The basilica at Ostia Antica (120) is such an example of a church originally built between persecutions: small, modest, with only a few token Christian symbols visible from outside. And just before the persecution of Decius, the "chapel" near the old entrance of the Priscilla Catacombs was extended; one can still see the steps linking the private house upstairs with the underground rooms (121).

In later centuries, Roman Christians tried to preserve the places where the great teachers, Peter and Paul, had taught. One such place, near the river Tiber, opposite the Trastevere quarter, is the church of San Paolo alla Regola (122). Tradition says it was here where Paul stayed for two years (Acts 28:30) and established a school. A more recent *hospitium et schola* (hospice and school) can now be seen (123), above first-century housing remains. It was here, say the Franciscans from Bombay, India, who guard the church today, that Paul "boldly and without hindrance preached the kingdom of God and taught about the Lord Jesus Christ" (Acts 28:31).

3. Christians and Jews

Who is Who?
Suetonius, Divus Claudius, 25:4

Since the Jews constantly made disturbances at the instigation of Chrestus, he (Claudius) expelled them from Rome.

A Case of Mixed Families?
Cassius Dio, Roman History 67,14:1-3

The same year, Domitian killed, along with many others, Flavius Clemens the consul. It didn't matter that he was a cousin and was married to Flavia Domitilla, who was also a relative of the emperor. The charge brought against both of them was atheism, a charge by which many others who drifted into Jewish ways were condemned. Some of these were put to death, and the rest were at least deprived of their property. Domitilla was merely banished to Pandateria. But Glabrio, who had been Trajan's colleague in the consulship, was put to death, having been accused of the same crimes as most of the others, and, in particular, of fighting as a gladiator with wild beasts.

Against the Theology of Aristotle
Galen

If I had in mind people who taught their pupils in the same way as the followers of Moses and Christ teach theirs — for they order them to accept everything on faith — I should not have given you a definition.

An Ostentatious Difference
Ignatius, To the Magnesians, 9:1-2

There are those of us who lived according to tradition but now have experienced newness of hope, no longer keeping the Sabbath, but living a life ruled by the Lord's day and knowing what it means to rise through him and his death. Of course, some deny this mystery, but through it we have received the power to believe, and therefore we endure that we may be disciples of Jesus Christ, our only Teacher. So how would we be able to live apart from him?

125

124

professions which would have put them in danger of having to break their Sabbath. In fact, the observance of the Sabbath was soon used in Roman literature as the stock example of what set the Jews (even those with Roman citizenship, and there were thousands of them) apart from the rest of the population. When Caesar was murdered, the Jews of Rome formed a procession to his funeral pyre.

Caesar's policies were continued under Augustus who allowed the Jews not to have to appear before the courts on a Sabbath; and he expressly permitted them to proselytize. By 64, while Paul was probably still (or again) in Rome, the Jews had become an important factor in Roman society. Poppaea, Nero's wife, was so pro-Jewish that she was called a "God-fearer," the technical term for someone who was close to conversion, observing the rules and regulations, without taking the last step. When Nero persecuted the Christians after the fire of Rome, he spared the Jews — fully aware (unlike some of his predecessors and successors) that the two communities and their theologies were separate.

When Paul came to Rome about AD 58, there were some 60,000 Jews living in the city. They had regrouped and reorganized themselves quickly after the death of Claudius (124) in AD 54, the year in which the expulsion edict of AD 49 had come to an end. For the Jews, this had not been the first expulsion from the city — there had been others in 139 BC and AD 19. However, it would be wrong to suggest that the Republic or the Empire were persistent in their desire to get rid of them. Julius Caesar, for example, actively protected them against the occasional outburst of anti-Judaism, permitting their rites to be performed openly. He authorized their annual contribution to the Temple in Jerusalem, exempted them from military service, and generally excused them from public duties or

The Ripple Effect

But in AD 70, when Titus destroyed Jerusalem, the ripples could be felt in Rome, too. The Arch of Titus, clearly visible to anyone who walked across the Forum (125), was built in honor of Titus's victory over the Jews and would remind Jews and Christians alike of the destruction of the place holy to them all.

After that, Jews in the empire faced turbulent times. Domitian, Trajan, and Hadrian suppressed them, and Hadrian did his best to make them rebel against him by prohibiting circumcision. The Bar Cochba Revolt, which ended in the second destruction of Jerusalem in AD 135, was — partly, at least — triggered by Hadrian's measure.

At the same time, leading Jewish scholars went to Rome, as they had always done when Paul met "the leaders of the Jews" (Acts 28:17). He certainly faced some of the most intelligent scholars of the old faith which had also been his.

Hadrian's edict was revoked after his death, but Jews were still not allowed to circumcise new converts. Septimius Severus, while persecuting Christians in North Africa with utmost severity, let Jews accede to high office in his administration.

126

127

Caracalla later enfranchised the Jews by the edict of 122, the *Constitutio Antoniana*. And Alexander Severus was so pro-Jewish that his opponents mockingly called him "Chief Rabbi."

The Jews in Rome had their synagogues; eleven are still known by name. Rome's harbor, Ostia, also had one, and remnants are still visible (126). The Jews had catacombs, six of which are known today. And they had quarters where they preferred to live, such as the area near the Porticus Octaviae (127), first built in 147 BC and reconstructed in AD 205. From 1558 to 1848, this densely populated Jewish quarter was turned into a ghetto. Some of the streets, like the Via della Reghinella (128), have hardly changed since those days, and in the walls of houses along the Via dell' Portico d'Ottavia, one can still see relics from Roman times, such as those at the house of Manilio (129). Today, the new synagogue of Rome, opened in 1904, overlooks the former ghetto opposite the Tiber Island (131), and the Jews have once more established themselves as citizens all over Rome (130).

Points of Contention

In the wake of Paul's only partly successful attempt at winning over the Roman Jews, both communities were certainly aware of what separated them. After the expulsion of Jews and Jewish Christians in AD 49 and the persecution of the Christians in AD 64/65, it remained an uneasy situation, punctuated by open conflict and hostility. In the first two texts quoted here, at the beginning of this chapter, we find authorities who tend to see the common roots and the Jewish origins of Christianity rather than the acute differences. And if a highly intelligent late second-century author like Galen from Pergamon, one of the great practicing doctors and medical philosophers of his time, regards the followers of Christ as people easily influenced by unthinking teachers, as compared to hard-boiled physicians and philosophers (like himself), he betrays the prejudice and arrogance of a man who very much prefers his own company and who is trying hard to avoid contact with worldviews differing from his own. Galen in fact

sounds just like one of those Athenian philosophers who brushed Paul's arguments aside with an off-hand "What is this babbler trying to say?" (Acts 17:18). To him, Judaism and Christianity are not to be taken all that seriously.

Could the Christians avoid being connected with their Jewish roots? The Jews tried to sever those bonds in the AD 90s, at Jamnia. One of their "Eighteen Benedictions" condemned the Christians as apostates: "May they be removed from the book of the living and not be inscribed among the just."

Christians were at first hesitant to retaliate. Ignatius, in his letter to the Magnesians of about AD 108, clearly states the superiority of the Christian faith. In the excerpt quoted here, at the beginning of this chapter, he mentions the dropping of the observance of the Sabbath as an outward sign of conversion to Christianity — a sign that even the pagan Romans understood, as bemused as they were by the Sabbath, the day on which nearly 60,000 people suddenly stopped tak-

130

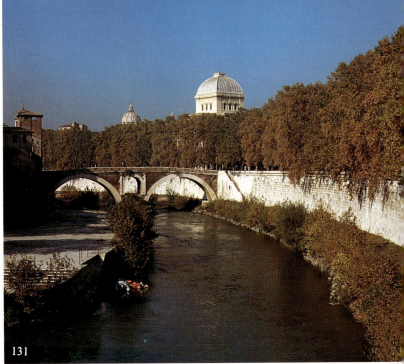

131

ing part in public life. But Ignatius makes his point theologically and refrains from any overt attack on Jewish attitudes towards the Christians.

Anti-Jewish?

Some have charged that parts of the New Testament are anti-Jewish (Luke, John, and sometimes Paul are the supposed culprits). But this theory does not stand up to proper analysis. Certainly John's Gospel accuses "the Jews" of acting against Jesus. But he himself was Jewish! We might compare him to a German resistance writer attacking the way his country followed Hitler's policy of persecuting Jews. Is such a writer anti-German?

It is true that Christians were forced to develop a theology as independent of their Jewish roots as possible, as soon as their attempts to take their fellow Jews with them into

132

he faith in Jesus as the Messiah had failed. They often did so with a strictness which left the Jewish Christians — who continued to exist, after all — in an unwelcome minority position. One should keep in mind, however, that the very Paul who has often been accused of preparing this slant almost single-handedly, spoke to the Jews, not to the Christians, when he addressed his first audience in Rome.

After Constantine's legalization of Christianity, the tone against the Jews became somewhat sharper. The church took a turn towards what became known as Christian "anti-semitism," of which the later ghettos are a direct result. In the first years of the fifth century, however, Rome's most important apse mosaic, in the church of Santa Pudenziana (132), still celebrated the twofold roots of the growing community. In the center is Christ enthroned, to his left and right are the apostles, among them Peter and Paul. And behind them are two women, one representing the "Church from the Circumcision," the other the "Church from the Gentiles." A few decades later, a wall mosaic in the church of Santa Sabina emphasizes the same point, and we are made to realize that there was a time when Christians knew (even if they did not always act accordingly) that the Jewish element in Christianity was not the weaker one, and certainly not inferior to the Gentile.

1. First Steps Towards Recognition

Galerius Changes Sides
Lactantius, On the Deaths of the Persecutors, 34

Among other arrangements, we are attempting to set all things right for the permanent advantage of the state according to the ancient laws and public order of the Romans. We've been especially concerned that Christians who left the teachings of their forefathers behind should return to a better mind. For some strange reason, these Christians had been willful and such folly possessed them that, instead of following the teaching of their ancestors, they were making their own laws according to their own judgment and pleasure, and, in the process, gaining a multitude of followers. In short, when our order was set forth that they should return to the ways of their ancestors, many of them were subdued by danger and exposed to jeopardy. Nevertheless, many were determined, neither offering worship and reverence to the gods but still worshipped the god of the Christians. We, therefore, because of our mild clemency and unbroken custom of granting pardon to all men, have thought it right in this case also to offer our speediest forgiveness, that Christians may exist again and establish their meeting houses as long as they do nothing contrary to good order. By another letter, we will instruct magistrates as to how they should proceed. Meanwhile, because of this forgiveness, it will be their duty to pray for us, the state, and themselves so that the commonwealth may endure unharmed on every side and that all may live securely in their habitations.

A Decisive Vision
Eusebius, Life of Constantine 28:1

Constantine was praying to his father's god, beseeching him to tell him who he was and imploring him to to stretch out his right hand to help him in his present difficulties. While he was fervently praying, an incredible sign appeared to him from heaven. (It would be hard to believe his account if it had been told by anyone else. But the victorious emperor long afterwards declared it to the writer of this history — when I was honored to meet and talk with him and he even confirmed his statement by an oath. Thus, who could doubt him, especially since time has established its truth?) He said that about noon, when the day was already beginning to decline, he saw with his own eyes the trophy of a cross of light in the heavens, above the sun, and an inscription that said "Conquer by This" attached to it. Seeing this, he and his army, which followed him on an expedition and witnessed the miracle, were struck with amazement.

He said that he doubted within himself what importance the vision might hold. He continued to ponder its meaning through until he fell asleep. While sleeping, the Christ of God appeared to him with the same sign he had seen earlier in the heavens. God commanded him to make a likeness of that sign which he had seen in the heavens and to use it as a safeguard in all encounters with his enemies.

134

135

133

When Diocletian issued the edict of
February 23, 303, which signaled the
beginning of his persecution of the
Christians, he had at his side a co-
signatory, a certain Maximinianus
Galerius. This Galerius was called a
"Caesar" (sort of a vice-emperor)
and adopted by Diocletian. He proved
an effective ally and heir. After the
abdication of Diocletian, he in-
tensified the cruelty of his measures.
Some of his regional "caesars," including Constantine, refused to co-
operate. In 310, Galerius became
mortally ill. A change of mind set in,
and he issued an edict of tolerance
which was made public April 30, 311.
For the first time in the history of the
empire, Christianity was made a
religio licita, a legal religion. Only a
few days after the edict, Galerius
died.

The long excerpt printed here at the
beginning of this chapter explains the
change in Galerius's attitude. It is
clear that he had not become a Christian himself, but his change of heart
came from recognizing the resilient
nature of Christianity. Since he could
not crush it, however hard he tried,

he realized that it would make much more sense to let its adherents worship their god and pray to this god "for our estate, and that of the state, and their own, that the commonwealth may endure on every side unharmed."

Lactantius

The Latin text of this edict is recorded in a fascinating "classic" of theological history, *De mortibus persecutorum* ("On the kinds of death of the persecutors"), written by Lactantius in 314-315. The author, a famous teacher of Latin rhetoric, had been summoned to Nicomedia by Emperor Diocletian. But soon he became a Christian and was forced to leave his teaching post and flee when the great persecution began. In the following years, he proved to be a theologian of high repute.

When the persecutions ceased, Lactantius was able to compile his book. A few years later, Constantine (now ruling the Western empire) remembered Lactantius and appointed him tutor to his son Crispus in Trier (in modern Germany). Constantine had a palace at Trier. Under its ruins, a giant ceiling painting has been found and carefully reconstructed. Among the many portraits in this painting, there are two men. One of them is thought to be Lactantius, either shown as a philosopher with a scroll, or as a bearded man with a wreath (134), a typical way of portraying rhetoricians. We cannot be sure that this man was Lactantius, but we do know that he was held in high regard by Constantine, who saw in him a living example of that breed of Christians who could combine classical learning with profound Christian thinking. In addition, Lactantius was a survivor of the last great persecution. He knew what was needed to make Christianity more and more approachable to the defenders of the traditional state religion(s). Thus, it is not unlikely that he was honored in this imperial painting along with other figures of the court. The portraits also include one of a young woman with a box of jewels, a laurel wreath and a halo − thought by some to be Constantine's wife, Maxima Fausta (135).

136

137

138

Constantine's Story

Constantine, born in 280, was brought up at the court of Diocletian, but did not actively participate in the persecution. His father, Constantius Chlorus, was a noted general and, for a time, one of the "caesars" under Galerius. When Constantius died in 306, young Constantine was declared "Augustus" by his troops. From his original power base in Britain and Gaul, Constantine built his influence with a series of political and military maneuvers. He signed an agreement with another "Augustus," Licinius (who ruled over the Asian part of the empire), and solidified his control of the Western empire. He centered his authority in Trier, where one of the old city gates, the Porta Nigra (literally, the "black gate") still reminds us of the glorious days when this was the capital from which the course of the lasting and thorough legalization of Christianity began (136).

Constantine's first step in this direction was, however, motivated by sheer power politics. There was only one thing which stood between him and power over Rome – Maxentius, an efficient ruler who tried to preserve Italy and Africa for himself despite Constantine's claims.

Maxentius was not anti-Christian; he revoked the edicts of Diocletian, handed back possessions to the Christian communities, and gave them the freedom to set up a church administration without state interference. At the same time, however, he increased his own veneration of Roman deities and traditions, singling out the two legendary founders of the city, Romulus and Remus, and the god of war, Mars.

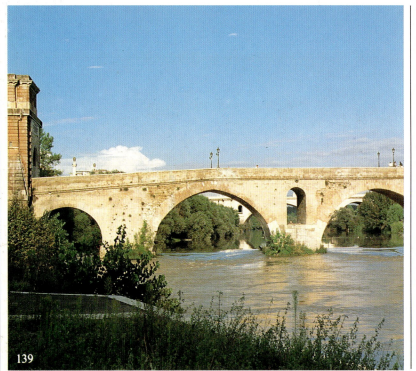

139

Conquer by This!

When Constantine assembled 40,000 troops and marched on Rome from Trier in 312, his motive therefore was certainly not one based on protecting the Christians against an active persecutor. But he had hardly left Trier when he had a curious vision. There are two surviving reports about this event, one in Latin by Lactantius, and one quoted here, at the beginning of this chapter, by Constantine's trusted church historian, Eusebius, in Greek.

Although neither Lactantius nor Eusebius mentions a particular site, tradition has it that on a wide plateau today called "Constantine's Height" and marked by a memorial cross (137), Constantine saw a cross of light in the sky with the inscription "Conquer by This!" Not far from the site, on the other side of the river Moselle, there is a memorial cross in front of the old church of the wine-

140

growing village of Piesport, inscribed with the Greek text of the vision (138). According to Eusebius, hours later Christ himself appeared to Constantine in a vision, commanding him to make a likeness of this sign for his army, "as a safeguard in all engagements with his enemies."

Constantine followed this command. We see him, in later frescoes and paintings, battling against Maxentius at the Milvian Bridge in Rome, the oldest Roman bridge still standing today (139), carrying with him the standard with the Cross of Christ and the "Chi-Rho" Emblem, signifying the first two letters of Christ's name in Greek (140).

After this victory, he refused to go to the Capitol — the custom for a victorious new ruler — but proceeded instead to encourage Christian institutions. It could be said that his final step along the path to Christianity was in 312, although he was not baptized until immediately before his death.

Maxentius, the loser, was subjected to a *damnatio memoriae*, a kind of condemnation of his legacy to oblivion. But Constantine nonetheless made good use of what he found in Rome, turning Maxentius's magnificent basilica into a basilica of his own. It overlooks the Forum, and although now in ruins, it still is one of the most impressive sights in Rome (141). As for the "Chi-Rho" symbol on Constantine's visionary cross, it became one of the most-repeated elements in early Christian art, often artistically stylized and sometimes together with symbols such as the doves of peace (142).

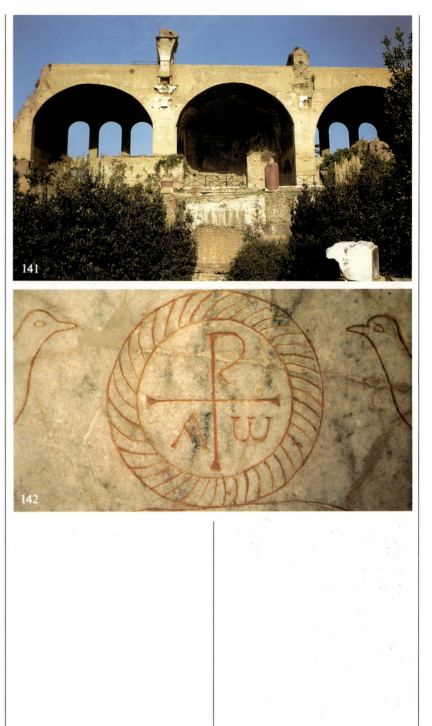

141

142

2. Consolidation

The Edict of Milan
Lactantius, On the Deaths of the Persecutors
48:2-9

We, Constantine Augustus and Licinius
Augustus, happily met at Milan to discuss the
things which concern the advantage and
security of the state. One thing we thought
would generally profit men and merited our
chief attention was the reverence paid to the
Divinity. Our purpose is to grant Christians and
all others the freedom to follow whatever worship they desire. In so doing, whatever Divinity
dwells in heaven may be benevolent and pro-
pitious to us and to those who are under our
authority. Therefore, we made our purpose
clear that no one should be refused complete
toleration whether he be a part of Christianity
or any other religion to which he feels most
suited. Our end hope is that the supreme
Divinity, whom we worship without compul-
sion, will continue to grant us his favor and
blessings in all things. It is our pleasure to
abolish all conditions regarding Christians that
were embodied in former orders. What
appeared inauspicious and foreign to our
Clemency should be abolished, and those who
wish to follow the ways of Christians may from
this moment do so freely and unconditionally
without being harassed or disquieted. We
thought it would be good to tell you in the
fullest manner that we have given free and
unreserved toleration to the Christians so that
they may freely practice their beliefs. When you
understand that we have granted this favor to the
Christians, you will understand that freedom is
granted to others, too. Their worship is likewise
left open and freely granted, as is fitting for our
quiet times, so that all may have complete
toleration in the practice of whatever worship he
has chosen. We have done this so that no
dimunition be made from the honor of any
religion.

Concerning the legal position of the Christians, we have thought fit to ordain the following. If any appear to have bought, whether from
our account or any other, the places at which
they formerly assembled, these shall be restored
to them without delay or doubtfulness and
without any payment or demand of price. Those
meeting places that have been obtained by gift
to the Christians shall also be restored without
delay in a similar manner. Regarding those who
have bought them or obtained them by a gift, if
they request anything of our benevolence, they
shall apply to the Vicarius that order may be
taken for them by our Clemency.

All these things must be delivered
immediately by your intervention to the cor-
poration of the Christians.

Imperial Greatness
Inscription on the Arch of Constantine

To the Emperor Caesar Flavius Constantine,
Maximus, Pius, Felix, Augustus, the Roman
Senate and People dedicated this arch,
decorated with his victories, because, by the
prompting of the Divinity, by the greatness of
his mind, he with his army, at one moment by a
just victory avenged the State both on the tyrant
and on all his party.

To the liberator of the city. To the establisher
of peace.

144

143

Christians, it still hesitates to place Christianity above the other religions of the empire.

Reconstruction

With this agreement, a thriving period of rebuilding and constructing of churches set in. Rebuilding meant going back to the house churches which had originally belonged to the Christian communities, repossessing the properties, and turning them into proper churches. This was the case with the majority of fourth- and fifth-century churches we still find in Rome and elsewhere. Constructing, however, sometimes meant turning the tables on the pagans by turning their shrines and temples into places of Christian worship.

Constantine was not quite averse to this procedure himself. For example, when he had the first church of St Peter built on the Vatican Hill between 324 and 326, he risked the wrath of his non-Christian subjects, including some influential senators, by choosing the steep slope of the hill alongside a road of tombs. He not only had to re-landscape that part of the hill, he also had to destroy a number of Roman tombs — sacrilege in the eyes of many non-Christian Romans. Traces of this demolition can still be seen in the excavations underneath the present-day church.

It was done, of course, because Constantine wanted to ensure that the church was

In February 312, Constantine and Licinius met in Milan and agreed to issue an agreement that would place Christianity unequivocally on a par with all other religions. A surviving version of this document, the first part of which is printed here, at the beginning of this chapter, was sent to the governor of the province of Bithynia (already well-known to us as a focal point of Christian activities) and distributed all over the empire. It was certainly due to Constantine's influence that religious policies were at the center of this writing. He had already prepared the

ground by sending several letters to African provinces, in which he strongly favored the Christians, requiring local administrators to hand back possessions to them and to grant them large amounts of money. It is apparent that Licinius and Constantine used the model of Galerius's edict of 311 as the basis for their instructions. But, comparing the documents, one soon realizes that, while theirs is even more outspokenly in favor of the

exactly above the tomb of Peter. And
the fact that he went to such extreme
lengths to achieve this end not only
indicates that there must have been
very hard evidence indeed for the site
of this tomb, but also that Constantine's devotion to the Christian faith
was firm enough to face the disgust
and enmity of leading Roman
families.

In some cases, the names of churches still betray their construction on
top of a pagan temple, like Santa
Maria in Aracoeli, on the Capitoline
Hill. Aracoeli, Altar of Heaven, refers
to a tradition which said that Emperor
Augustus had erected an altar here to
the firstborn god, after a prophecy
told him that a divine child, son of a
virgin, would be born and would
topple the altars of the gods. On the
site of Augustus's altar, Helena, the
mother of Constantine, was buried,
and her tomb is still shown in the
church standing there today.

In the Forum, too, pagan sites were
put to Christian use. Late, but visually impressive, are the church of Santi
Cosma e Damiano, which was built
into a "Temple of the Holy City"
erected by Emperor Vespasian, and
the Temple of Antoninus Pius and
Faustina, erected after that emperor's
death in 161 and later turned into the
church of San Lorenzo in Miranda
(143). The old inscription honoring
the "divine Antoninus" and his
equally "divine" wife Faustina can
still be seen today (144). All this
happened after Constantine's time,
but the spirit of taking possession, of
usurping what had belonged to the
old suppressors, was truly instigated
by Constantine himself.

The Imperial Tradition

It must be said that Constantine
was not a meek and humble Christian. He still stood in the tradition of
the great emperors. The giant statue
of himself which he had erected is
still awe-inspiring in its shattered

145

146

147

remnants (145). In another statue, he was said to have been depicted with that famous visionary Cross in his right hand. Eusebius writes in his *Church History* (9,9:10-11) that it was "the saving sign, the true proof of steadfastness." Modern scholarship regards this as a reference to the *labarum*, the military standard with the Christian monogram which was commonly used in the army after Constantine. There is a copy of this statue, proud in triumph, at the old main entrance to the church of San Giovanni in Laterano, but unfortunately, the uplifted right hand is empty.

After Constantine's victory at the Milvian Bridge, the Senate of Rome erected a monumental arch in his honor (146), with the dedicatory inscription preserved and printed here in full, at the beginning of this chapter. The arch is decorated with scenes from Roman history and legend, from victorious battles, mostly as spoils from other arches and monuments, and it shows scenes from Constantine's own life, even with him depicted sacrificing to pagan gods. It has irritated Christian interpreters that such pre-conversion scenes are represented, whereas no Christian symbols are visible. One

has to remember, however, that this is not Constantine's own statement but an arch presented to him by the still mainly non-Christian senate in 315. It may well be that the statue with the *labarum*, which he had erected himself, was meant to supplement what is missing here. It is all the more interesting that the Invincible Sun God, *Sol Invictus*, singled out on the arch itself, was also a term actually used by Constantine quite consciously. This god had been his symbol even before the battle at the Milvian Bridge. Instead of just dropping it on conversion, he reinterpreted it. Fully and correctly understood, the true god of the sun was none other than Jesus Christ himself: "His face was like the sun shining in all its brilliance," as it says in Revelation 1:16, or again in Psalm 84:11: "For the Lord God is a sun and a shield." In the Vatican graveyard, there is a Christian tomb vault which also makes this connection quite unmistakably: here, Christ is shown as Helios, the Greco-Roman sun god. The historical Christ had finally replaced the pagan deity.

The Church organized itself quickly under Constantine. Buildings like Santa Prisca on the Aventine Hill (147),

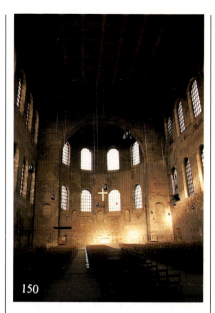

150

inconspicuous from outside, house-churches from as early as the first, second and third centuries, were used as administrative seats, linking tradition with strategic concepts of how to run a growing institution effectively.

And Constantine remembered Trier, where it had all begun for him. Between 321 and 326, he built an enormous basilica, parts of which are still integrated into the Romanesque cathedral that stands there today. Excavations have yielded many traces of his construction work, more magnificent than any church he built in Rome. The assembly and audience hall at his palace in Trier has remained more or less intact and was restored in the 19th century (149). Often called "Constantine's Basilica" today, it never was a church in his own time. (In fact "basilica" originally does not refer to a church at all, but merely to a "hall.") It became a Protestant church in the 19th century and is still used as such (150). But it is safe to assume that Constantine himself would have approved of such an integration of imperial grandeur with the veneration of the victorious Savior God, here at Trier more than anywhere else.

149

3. Towards a State Religion

The Emperor as Bishop
Eusebius, Life of Constantine 4:24

It was not without reason that once, while entertaining a company of bishops, Constantine used the expression "that he himself too was a bishop." He addressed them (in my hearing) in the following words: "You are bishops whose jurisdiction is within the Church; I also am a bishop, ordained by God to overlook those outside the Church." And truly his actions matched his words, for he watched over all his subjects with an episcopal care and exhorted them as much as he could to follow a godly life.

The Empire Turns Christian
Eusebius, Oration on the Tricennalia of Constantine, 2:4-5

He who is the pre-existent Word, the Savior of all things, imparts to his followers the seeds of true wisdom and salvation. He makes them wise and helps them understand the kingdom of their Father. Our emperor, his friend who interprets the Word of God, aims to bring the whole human race back to the knowledge of God. He clearly proclaims with a powerful voice the laws of truth and godliness to all who dwell on the earth. Once more, the universal Savior opens the heavenly gates of his Father's kingdom to those who are straying from his way. Our emperor, who emulates his Divine example, having purged his earthly dominion from every stain of impious error, invites each holy and pious worshipper within his imperial mansion. He earnestly desires to save with all its crew that mighty vessel of which he is the appointed pilot.

An Imperial Baptism
Eusebius, Life of Constantine, 4:62-64

When the emperor Constantine was baptized, the Church officers performed the sacred ceremony in the customary manner. Constantine was first given the required instructions before he received the mystic ordinance. Thus was Constantine the first of the Roman emperors who was known to become a converted Christian and received into full participation in the Church dedicated to the martyrs of Christ. Having been gifted with the Divine seal of baptism, renewed, and filled with heavenly light, his soul rejoiced because of his fervent faith, and he was astonished at the manifestation of the power of God.

When the baptismal ceremony was over, Constantine dressed in shining imperial clothes. They seemed bright as light. He reclined on a couch of pure white and refused to clothe himself in the customary purple garment of the emperor any more.

After thanking God, he completed various secular arrangements and died on Whitsunday.

Coins of Constantine, minted during the later years of his reign, show him with Christian symbols or with his eyes turned heavenwards, as we see in the surviving head of a giant statue in Rome (151). Constantine knew that Jesus Christ, who ascended into heaven, was a figure of history, not just a legendary deity like all the others he had previously venerated. And the historical Jesus had lived in the Holy Land, had been crucified, had risen, and had ascended in Jerusalem. Jerusalem, then, became a focus of Constantine's attention. Above the very sites of the crucifixion, and the empty tomb, he built the church of the Holy Sepulchre (152). As early as 324, he had allowed the bishop of Jerusalem, Makarios, to remove the Roman Temple of Venus from the site of the empty tomb. His mother, Helena, visited the Holy Land in 326, finding all sorts of

152

153

151

relics, which she took back with her to Rome. And on the strength of her reports, the church was built and dedicated in 335.

Quite a few other churches were built on sites venerated by Christians at the instigation of Helena. With these activities, the cradle of Christianity was fully integrated into an increasingly Christian empire. When Constantine established another capital city, on the site of the old Byzantium Constantinople, in 326, one of the first major buildings erected there was a church. It would later become known as *Hagia Sophia*. Constantine's structure burned but was rebuilt by Justinian in 532–537. This magnificent church remained a wonder and the symbol of Eastern Christendom for centuries. *Hagia Sophia* is now a museum in modern Turkish Istanbul with islamic signs prominently displayed within. Nevertheless it stands today as an awe-inspiring survivor of the Christian past and its amazing dome is still studied by architects who consider it a theoretical impossibility.

The Emperor as Bishop

With the empire gaining more and more of a Christian image, the emperor had to concern himself with the adaptation of state administration in terms of Christian thinking. "You are bishops whose jurisdiction is within the Church," he told a group of bishops, in a source quotation printed here, at the beginning of the chapter, "I also am a bishop, ordained by God to overlook those outside the Church," he added.

Consequently, internal state matters became Christianized, too, as we can gather from the second text printed here. While Constantine still had to accomodate non-Christians in a situation where Christianity had not been declared the one and only state religion, he did his best to set a trend in motion.

154

155

Adjacent to the Lateran Basilica in Rome (154), which was a private palace which he gave to the pope in 312, is the baptistry of San Giovanni in Fonte (155). It was built by Constantine above a pagan *Nymphaeum*. An impressive octagonal building, it highlights the importance attributed by this emperor to the basic Christian "initiation rite." In fact, Constantine considered the purification of baptism so important, that he did not want to negate it for himself with any future sins. This attitude may seen odd to modern minds, but it was common in the fourth century (though Constantine did not recommend it to the Church at large). As the emperor of the whole empire, he may have felt that this should be the fitting conclusion to his life — another, final sign to the outside world that he died as a convinced Christian. It has indeed been assumed by scholars that he intended to die not in the traditional imperial purple, but in the white baptismal cloak, reserving the forgiving power of baptism to the moment when no sins could be committed afterwards, and no further sacrament of penance would be required.

The scene of his baptism in 337 is beautifully depicted in a medieval fresco at the church of Santi Quattro Coronati (153). Baptistries became focal points of church architecture. Early examples from Constantine's century range in style from the first baptistry found north of the Alps, underneath the Cathedral of Saint Pierre in Geneva (156) to Kourion on the island of Cyprus in the Mediterranean (157).

The Mighty Vessel

Constantine steered the ship of the Empire, "that mighty vessel of which he is the appointed pilot," as Euse-

bius quotes in his text printed here, at the beginning of this chapter, slowly but surely toward state religion. The symbol of the ship, reminiscent of the boats used by Jesus and the disciples on the Sea of Galilea, depicted in a contemporary mosaic from Magdala (159), was one of the many Christian symbols used to replace the old Roman ones like the eagle (158), which had begun to lose its original splendor.

New Problems

"Success" brings its own kind of problems. For the Church, prestige and power proved more precarious than the pressure of persecution. The Church spread more rapidly than it ever had before. It became easier, indeed fashionable, to become a Christian. Accommodations were made to the pagan pasts of the new members. And sad to say, the Church, which had known such prolonged oppression, did not shrink from becoming an oppressor once in power.

Was Constantine a Christian?

Was Constantine truly a Christian or just a political opportunist who saw the Christian movement as the wave of the future, a good ally for his ambitions? Why did he put off his baptism until just before his death in 337? Some see him as God's appointed agent for the Church. They remind us of his great contributions to Christianity. For instance, in 325 he convened and presided over the Council of Nicea, an important council that checked heresy and defined orthodox doctrine. Beyond any doubt, he took great personal risks in his espousal of Christianity. However, others see him as the catalyst that plunged the Church into a sad departure from biblical faith and practice.

159

160

158

"Constantinian Christianity" provided benefits that have blessed the Church down to our own day. But it also brought many temptations and raised questions about the true nature of the Church. Some of these problems we are still facing.

But before he and the Church reached this stage, they rejoiced in what Raphael so aptly reproduced in a painting on a ceiling in the Vatican (160): the downfall of the pagan gods before the cross of Jesus, the triumph of the trial and testimony of the early Church.